The Eye Cannot Say
to the Hand,
"I Have No Need of You"

*An inspiring study of St. Paul's comparison of the members of the
church to the members of the human body (1 Cor. 12:4-30).*

*There are no passengers on spaceship earth.
We are all crew.*

— *Marshall McLuhan*

Light & Life Publishing Company
Minneapolis, Minnesota

Light & Life Publishing Company
P.O. Box 26421
Minneapolis, MN 55426-0421

Copyright © 2005
Light & Life Publishing Company

ISBN 1-880971-95-X

First Corinthians 12:4-30

Now there are varieties of gifts, but the same Spirit: and there are varieties of service, but the same Lord; and there are varieties of working, but it is the same God who inspires them all in every one. To each is given the manifestation of the Spirit for the common good. To one is given through the Spirit the utterance of wisdom, and to another utterance of knowledge according to the same Spirit, to another faith by the same Spirit, to another gifts of healing by the one Spirit, to another the working of miracles, to another prophecy, to another the ability to distinguish between spirits, to another various kinds of tongues, to another the interpretation of tongues. All these are inspired by one and the same Spirit, who apportions to each one individually as he wills. For just as the body is one and has many members and all the members of the body, though many, are one body, so it is with Christ. For by one spirit we were all baptized into one body—Jews or Greeks, slaves or free—and all were made to drink of one Spirit. For the body does not consist of one member but of many. If the foot should say, "Because I am not a hand, I do not belong to the body," that would not make it any less a part of the body. And if the ear should say, "Because I am not an eye, I do not belong to the body," that would not make it any less a part of the body. If the whole body were an eye, where would be the hearing? If the whole body were an ear, where would be the sense of smell? But as it is, God arranged the organs in the body, each one of them as he chose. If all were a single organ, where would the body be? As it is, there are many parts, yet one body. The eye cannot say to the hand, "I have no need of you," nor again the head to the feet, "I have no need of you." On the contrary, the parts of the body which seem to be weaker are indispensable, and those parts are treated with greater modesty, which our more presentable parts do not require. But God has so composed the body, giving the greater honor to the inferior part, that there may be no discord in the body, but that the members may have the same care for one another. If one member suffers, all suffer together; if one member is honored, all rejoice together. Now you are the body of Christ and individually members of it. And God has appointed in the church first apostles, second prophets, third teachers, then workers of miracles, then healers, helpers, administrators, speakers in various kinds of tongues. Are all apostles? Are all prophets? Are all teachers? Do all work miracles? Do all possess gifts of healing? Do all speak with tongues? Do all interpret? But earnestly desire the higher gifts.

Table of Contents

PART ONE: WHAT DOES IT MEAN TO BE MEMBERS OF THE BODY OF CHRIST?

PART TWO: LAITY AND HIERARCHY: THEIR RESPECTIVE ROLES AS MEMBERS OF THE BODY OF CHRIST

PART THREE: SYNDIACONIA, THE SHARED ROLE OF THE HIERARCHY AND LAITY IN THE CHURCH

.

PART ONE

What does it mean to be members of the Body of Christ?

DO NOT DEPRIVE THE BODY OF ITS MEMBERS

We read in a third century Syrian document, *The Didaskalia,*

> *When you are teaching, command and exhort the people to be faithful to the assembly of the church. Let them not fail to attend, but let them gather faithfully together. Let no one deprive the church by staying away: by so doing they deprive the Body of Christ of one of its members.... Do not, then, make light of your own selves, do not deprive the Body of Christ of his members; do not rend, do not scatter, his Body.*

When we say that we are going to church, it means that we are going to the assembly of the faithful, not just for individual prayer but in order, together with all the faithful, to *constitute the church,* to be what we became on the day of our baptism—*members*, in the fullest, absolute meaning of the term—*members of the Body of Christ.* "You are the body of Christ and individually members of it" (1 Cor. 12:27). We go to church to *constitute* the church, to be living, active members of the body through which Christ works today, to be "a holy nation, a royal priesthood, a chosen race" (1 Peter 2:9-10)—to manifest and confess the presence of Christ and His kingdom in the world, to "declare the wonderful deeds of Him who called us out of darkness into light".

REMAINING ALIVE AND VITAL IN THE BODY

We remain alive and vital only as long as we remain in the body. For example, if a finger is severed from the body, it loses its life and dies. So it is with Christians. We are alive only as long as we remain in the Body. If we cut ourselves off from the Body, the Holy Spirit is no longer with us. We die spiritually. "I am the vine, you are the branches" (John 15:1-6), said Jesus. If we abide in Christ and maintain our connection with Him, we shall experience true *koinonia*: a real connection with Him and with each other as members of the one Body of Christ, feeling each other's pain, rejoicing in one another's joy, etc. This kind of *koinonia* or *communion* is made possible only as we truly abide in Him, and He in us, in His Body, the Church.

REMAINING CONNECTED

There are many people who have paralyzed legs. In many cases, there's nothing wrong with the legs, but the nerves to the legs have been severed or damaged. The nerves leading from the brain are no longer connected to the legs. The same thing often happens to Christians. They are spiritually cut off from the Head, Jesus. The result is paralysis. Many times the physically paralyzed can walk again if the severed nerve can be re-connected to the control center through surgery. In like manner, if we separate ourselves from the Body of Christ through sin, God's grace re-integrates us into the Body through repentance and confession. "Have you committed a sin?" asks

St. John Chrysostom, "then enter the Church and repent of your sin … for here is the Physician, not the Judge; here one is not investigated but receives remission of sins."

THE UMBILICAL CORD

How do we maintain our connection to God? When we are born, the umbilical cord that connected us to our mother for sustenance and life is severed. But there is another umbilical cord that should never be severed. It is the spiritual umbilical cord, the umbilical cord of faith, Baptism and the Eucharist, by which we remain connected to God for sustenance, wisdom, strength, spirit and life.

It is when we sever this spiritual umbilical cord through pride, disobedience and sin that life with God begins to die in us. It is then that we lose meaning and become bored with life. Jesus came to give us a new connection to God. In fact, He is our new umbilical cord. As He said, "I am the vine, you are the branches. He who abides in me and I in him, he it is that bears much fruit, for apart from me you can do nothing" (John 15:5). "In Him was life, and the life was the light of men," wrote the Apostle John (John 1:4).

The importance of keeping the spiritual umbilical cord to God connected explains why Jesus called for repentance in His very first sermon. For, it is through daily repentance that the cord, when severed by sin, is reconnected to the source of life.

Julian of Norwich, the 14th century English mystic, pictured Jesus as carrying us within Himself as a mother carries a child in her womb. The exact words of Julian were, "Our Savior is our true Mother, in whom we are endlessly born and out of whose womb we shall never come. In His motherhood of mercy and grace...our precious...Jesus feeds us with Himself...with the blessed Sacrament (the Eucharist)." "He who eats my flesh and drinks my blood abides in me and I in Him" (John 6:56).

The umbilical cord by which He feeds us is never severed by God—only by man's free will through sin. Such is the awesome power God bestowed upon us when He endowed us with the gift of free will.

It is through this spiritual umbilical cord of faith and the sacraments that each member of the Body of Christ remains connected to the life-giving vine, Jesus, to bear much fruit for Him.

Remaining connected to Christ establishes a sense of *koinonia* in the Body of Christ. It establishes a communion of love and truth, which is the expression for the Kingdom of God in our midst. Alexis Khomiakov was fond of describing the Church as "an organic community of love". The image of the members of the body that St. Paul uses is a wonderful example of how such *koinonia* operates.

THE OLD WOMAN AND THE ONION

The opposite of *koinonia* (communion) is isolation. This is exemplified by Dostoevsky's story of the old woman and the onion. You may remember how her guardian angel tried to pull the old woman out of the lake of fire with the help of an onion that she had once given to a beggar. When the other people in the lake crowded around her, hoping to be pulled out as well, she exclaimed with indignation: "Let go, it's me who's being pulled out, not you. It's my onion, not yours!" As soon as she spoke those words, the onion broke in two and she fell back into the lake of fire; for in her unwillingness to share, in her refusal to say, "It's our onion," she chose isolation rather than *koinonia*. The same point is made in one of the basic texts of Orthodox monasticism, the *Gerontikon* or *Sayings of the Desert Fathers*. It is said that when St. Makarios the Egyptian asked the skull of a pagan priest what kind of torment the condemned were suffering in hell, the priest replied, "We cannot look at each other face to face, but we are each fixed back to back." Then he added, "But when you pray for us, each of us can see the other's face a little." The opposite of *koinonia* is isolation or individualism.

IDIOTIS OR PROSOPON?

In Greek there are two words for person. One is *atomon*. The word "atomon" means a person who has isolated himself. He does not relate to people. He is impersonal. He lives by himself. He is an *idiotis* in Greek, which is the derivation of the English word *idiot*. It describes a loner, one who keeps to himself and avoids people, living alone as in a remote shack somewhere in Montana.

The other word for person in Greek is *prosopon*. It is derived from two Greek words: *pros* which means toward and *opsin* which means face.

Literally, it means "looking into another's face or eyes." It expresses the truth that we become persons as we live in relationship to God and other people. Relationships are central to our lives. Our learning, our work, the discovery of ourselves—all depend on relationships. We cannot truly know ourselves if we do not have other people to whom we can relate. It is interesting that the word *prosopon* which means person, also means one's face in Greek. In other words, it is only as I "face" another person, look into his eyes, relate to him, that I myself become a person and come to understand who I am. No one can become a person alone.

Thus it is that God created us to live in relationship to Him and other people. He created us to live in a special *koinonia* or communion which St. Paul describes as the Body of Christ.

THE OPPOSITE OF KOINONIA: INDIVIDUALISM

The opposite of the *koinonia*, the communion that we see in the Body of Christ, is isolation and individualism, an individualism which says, "I am sovereign. I am self-sufficient. I don't need anybody." This is the individualism that St. Paul described when he talked about the eye saying to the hand, "I have no need of you." Individualism, by the way, was the original sin when, in effect, Adam said to God, "I will eat of the tree of the knowledge of good and evil and I will surpass you. I will be god. I don't need you."

"The deepest truth about ourselves is neither that we are self-sufficient nor that we are weak, needy, and fallible; it is that we are created for communion with God, with one another, and with the whole Creation…. Yet human beings have persistently rejected, and continue to reject, that communion."*

THE KOINONIA OF THE HOLY TRINITY

The beautiful *koinonia* that exists in the Body of Christ on earth (so well described by St. Paul) is but a reflection of the *koinonia* that exists in the Holy Trinity where the Three Persons work together in utmost harmony and love. God the Father would never think of saying to the Son, "I have no need of You." And the Son would never dream of saying to the Father, or the Holy Spirit to the Father and the Son, "I have no need of you." That would be individualism. The Trinity is the opposite of individualism. It is *koinonia*, community, harmony, fellowship, communion, love. It is all the members of the body working together in love, "in honor preferring one another," as St. Paul says. Just as it is nonsensical to think of the Father, Son and Holy Spirit as isolated individuals, so it is a contradiction to think of a Christian as an isolated individual, sufficient unto himself. To participate in the Eucharist is to be a person in communion (*koinonia*) with the Trinity and the other members of the Body of Christ. It is interesting to note that in Greek the Eucharist is referred to as *theia koinonia* (Divine Communion).

Robert Bellah, the prominent University of California sociologist, reported that a frightening phenomenon is re-

---

* *Embodying Forgiveness*. L. Gregory Jones. Eerdmans Publ. Co. Grand Rapids, MI. 1995.

emerging in North American society and taking over the rugged individualist of the late nineteenth century, responsible to no one but himself. More than that, Bellah concluded that the one institution which ought to be a counterforce to rugged individualism is the church, which claims to be a social body whose members are dependent upon one another for life in the spirit, especially in view of the doctrine of St. Paul of a single body in which no one member can say to another, "I have no need of you" (1 Cor. 12:21). Yet Bellah believes that even the church, instead of influencing American society, is being influenced by it, becoming more and more individualistic. And when I say the Church I mean each one of us, with all the emphasis and attention on *me* and *mine*.

Even when it comes to worship, many of the laity merely "attend", while the ordained clergy "celebrate" the liturgy. This is not what the liturgy is all about. It is the people of God—all the members of the body—who celebrate the liturgy together. No one "attends". If one does, he or she cuts oneself off from the body. This is how individualism dismembers the body.

ST. BASIL ON THE DEFICIENCIES OF THE SOLITARY LIFE

St. Basil launches a long attack on the solitary life of the monks in the seventh of his *Longer Rules*. Living alone was a dangerous temptation for St. Basil since the purpose of the Christian life is love, whereas the solitary life has one aim, serving the needs of the individual, which is "plainly in conflict with the law of love".

"Whose feet will you then wash?" asks St. Basil. "Whom will you care for? In comparison with whom will you be last if you live by yourself?" He goes on to say that the solitary will have no one to correct him for his deficiencies. For St. Basil, the most serious drawback for the solitary is that one will not be able to share his spiritual gifts with others. Nor will he be able to benefit from the gifts of others. For these reasons, St. Basil favors life lived in community. He realized that ecclesiologically, theologically and eucharistically, "we are members one of another".

Both in the throne-room of heaven as well as all about us in the Body of Christ, we are surrounded by a "great cloud of witnesses" (Hebrews 2:1). We cannot possess the Spirit in isolation, only as members of the Body of Christ. The gifts of the Holy Spirit are given not to individuals but to persons in communion. When you become a Christian, you need the gifts of the other Christians in the Church, just as they need yours. Metropolitan John Zizioulias expressed this well when he wrote,

> ...the Holy Spirit is the bond of love and wherever
> he "blows" he does not create good individual
> Christians but persons in communion with God
> and with one another, i.e., he creates a community.
> It is in this sense that it remains a fundamental and
> irrefutable truth that the Spirit exists only in the
> Church, the community par excellence, the Body of
> Christ, and that all spiritual gifts, such as inspira-
> tion, charisma, ministry, etc. cannot be conceived
> as possessions of individuals, but can exist only in

persons in communion, i.e., in the context of the ecclesial [Church] community. *

In this age of hypermodern individualism we need to remember that we are "body parts" of Jesus, living members of His Body, animated by the Holy Spirit. Writing about what it means to receive the Body of Christ in the Eucharist, Blessed Augustine wrote,

The faithful know and receive the Body of Christ if they labor to be the body of Christ; and they become the body of Christ if they study to live by the Spirit of Christ: for that which lives by the Spirit of Christ is the body of Christ.

WE PRAY NOT AS ISOLATED INDIVIDUALS BUT AS GOD'S FAMILY

Koinonia is established by remaining connected to God—Father, Son and Holy Spirit through His word, prayer and the Eucharist. Through baptism we become members of the Body of Christ and of one another. We become responsible for one another. We become members of God's huge family called the Communion of Saints, some in heaven and some on earth (Eph. 3:14). As members of such a huge family, we do not pray alone. We pray together with the Theotokos and the saints. When we worship, we who constitute the Body of Christ here on earth, join the innumerable company of angels, saints, and

* *Appendix—The Authority of the Bible.* The Ecumenical Review Vol. XXI, No. 2, April 1969.

loved ones in heaven. Together with them, we bow down and worship the Father, the Son, and the Holy Spirit (Eph. 3:18). We pray not as isolated individuals but as a *koinonia*, as members of God's family, that on earth as well as that in heaven. This is true *koinonia*, or communion. "You are the body of Christ and individually members of it" (1 Cor. 12:27). And every member of the body serves and glorifies Christ in and through one's body.

In the words of St. John Chrysostom,

> *Let the eye look on no evil thing, and it has become a sacrifice; let your tongue speak nothing filthy, and it has become an offering; let your hand do no lawless deed, and it has become a whole burnt offering.... Let us then from our hands and feet and mouth and all other members, yield a first-fruit to God.*

As members of the body, we are dependent upon the head (Christ) and upon each other. "We, though many, are one body in Christ, and individually members of one another" (Rom. 12:5). The varieties of gifts given to us are for the benefit of the one body, so that everything be done in love for the building up of the one body.

"SUPPOSE YOU SLIP THROUGH HIS FINGERS"

A little girl was sharing one day what Jesus meant to her. She concluded by quoting these comforting words of Jesus: "And I give unto them eternal life; and they shall never perish, neither shall any man pluck them out of my hand" (John 10:29). Just then a doubting friend came up with the question, "But suppose you slip through His fingers?" Quick as a flash, she replied, "Never, never! You see, I am one of His fingers."

This little girl had caught the meaning of St. Paul's words in 1 Cor. 12:4-30. That great biblical principle had lodged in her heart; namely, that "we are members of His body, of His flesh, and of His bones" (Eph 5:30). She knew that she had been joined inseparably to Jesus and that she was attached to Him. Her fingers were now indeed the fingers of Jesus. They belonged to Him; they were consecrated to Him; they were dedicated to serve Him.

When St. Symeon the New Theologian had returned from church one day where he had received Communion, he sat down and meditated on what had happened to his body as a result of his receiving the Body and Blood of Jesus. These hands, he mused, these feet, these eyes, these ears, so frail, so powerless, are the hands, the feet, the eyes, the ears of Christ. This body, so mean, so old, is the place of the divine presence. We are not just *disconnected* hands and feet, eyes and limbs. We are *connected* as members of His Body, animated and vivified by the breath of His Spirit. "I am the vine, you are the branches. He who abides in Me, and I in him, bears much fruit; for without me you can do nothing" (John 15:5).

Seeing a person coming down the street, one devout believer said, "Make way! Make way! Here comes the image of God. Here comes the living icon of God." He could just as well have said, "Here comes the Body of Christ." We are indeed, as St. Paul says, "members of His body, of His flesh, and of His bones" (Eph. 5:30).

WHAT DOES THE WORD "MEMBER" MEAN?

When we speak of the grace of God working through the Church, we must remember that as members of His Body, we are the Church. We are individually members of His Body. "Now you are Christ's body, and each of you a limb or organ of it" (1 Cor. 12:27).

When we use the word "member" today, we usually mean a person who belongs to a debating club or a political party. Members in such groups are a collection of individuals who happen to have joined an organization. But St. Paul uses the word member (*melos*) in an organic sense. We are members of Christ as the eye, ear, hand, and feet are members of the body. It is a living, organic communion of love and truth with Christ and with each other.

"WE ARE YOUR HEART"

Shortly before his death, Dr. Tom Dooley, a missionary physician, returned to the United States to raise funds for his hospital in Southeast Asia. As a physician he knew he had terminal cancer and would not live long. But his main concern was that his medical work would continue after his death.

While he was in America, a telegram arrived from some of the medical personnel he had trained to be his helpers in the mission hospital. The message read: "We need you here. But while you are gone, we are the fingers of your flesh to heal the sick. We are your ears to hear their cries of pain. We are your heart to love them."

Isn't this what Jesus asks each of us to do? We are His hands on this earth to heal the sick, to set the prisoner free, to restore sight to the blind. We are His ears to hear their cries of pain and despair. We are His heart to love them. He has no heart or hands but ours with which to do His work in the world today. "We are members of His body, of His flesh, and of His bones" (Eph. 5:30).

GOD CHOOSES A BODY

When God desired to work among us in this world, He took onto Himself a human body like ours. We call this the Incarnation: God taking on a body and living among us. With and through that body God acted during the thirty-three years that He lived in this world. He taught, He healed, He forgave, He offered Himself on the Cross for our salvation. Then on Ascension Day, His body left the earth, and He was no longer physically active among us.

If God intended, after the Ascension, to do more work among us, He had either to bring that body back again (as He will do when He comes at the Last Judgment), or else He had to use some other body. He chose to do the latter, i.e., to make use of some other body. He chose to work through the Body of believers: "You are Christ's body." All those Christians who have been baptized, who have received the Holy Spirit and share in the life of Christ through the Eucharist, make up the Body that is the instrument of Christ's work on earth today. In other words, Christ lives in all of us who share His life through

Baptism and the Eucharist. He continues to work and act through us who make up His body in the world—the Church.

When Saul was on the road to Damascus to arrest Christians, he was zapped by a light from heaven and he heard a voice saying, "Saul, Saul, why are you persecuting me?" (Acts 9:1-9). Isn't it strange that Saul who had never seen Jesus was being accused of persecuting Him? Saul answered, "Who are you, Lord?" The answer came, "I am Jesus, whom you are persecuting." We note in this incident how the person of Jesus and the body of believers are identified as a single entity. When Paul was persecuting the Christians, he was persecuting Christ, "Saul, Saul, why are you persecuting *me*?" In persecuting the Body of Christ, the Christians, Saul was persecuting Christ Himself. "You are the body of Christ and individually members of it" (1 Cor. 12:27).

THE ON-GOING INCARNATION

The Incarnation of Jesus was not a thirty-three year experiment by God in history, a one-shot physical incursion into our lives. The incarnation began with Jesus, and it has never ended. God's Body is still in our midst. We are the Body of Christ. This is not just a metaphor. St. Paul states it plainly, "We *are* Christ's body."

The body of believers, like the Eucharist, is the Body of Christ in an organic sense. It is not just a mystical reality but a physical one; not something that represents Christ, it is Christ. Thus it is true that we just don't go to church; we *are* the church wherever we go. "When does the liturgy begin?" someone asked. He was told, "It begins when you leave church and go back into the world to be the church, to be the Body of Christ, to celebrate 'the liturgy after the liturgy'."

CHRIST IS STILL IN OUR MIDST THROUGH HIS BODY

This has tremendous implications. It means that the Incarnation of God in Christ did not end after thirty-three years, when Jesus ascended to the Father. He is still here. He continues to dwell among us in the body of believers. Through the sacraments of Baptism, Chrismation, and the Eucharist, we have become Christ's mystical and physical presence in the world today, i.e., His hands, feet, ears, eyes, mind and heart. As God once acted through Jesus, so He now acts through us, the members of His Body. "You are the body of Christ and individually members of it" (1 Cor. 12:27).

DO I BURN WITH LOVE FOR THE MEMBERS OF HIS BODY?

If I really believe this, then I should ask myself some questions, such as: As the foot of Christ's Body, do I use my feet to visit the sick, the bereaved, the unfortunate? As the hand of Christ, do I use my hands to give assistance when and where it is needed? As the ear of Christ, do I use my ears to listen compassionately to those who are hurting? As the eye of Christ, do I use my eyes to see the needs about me and try to help? As the voice of

Christ, do I use my voice to bear witness to Him, to offer comfort to a sobbing child, a widowed mother, a bereaved friend, a lonely senior?

If the Church is the Body of Christ, it must have a heart burning with love, for God is love. Does my heart—your heart—burn with love for God's people? If it burns with love for God, it will certainly burn with love for God's people.

OUR PRAYERS NEED FLESH AND BONES

This means that my outreach to the other members of the body must be *incarnational*. If my mother is sick and I pray that she gets better but do not drive her to see a doctor, I have not given any *incarnational* flesh and bones to my prayer. If a friend looks depressed and I pray for her, but do not visit her or phone her, my prayer is not *incarnational*. It lacks skin and bones. True prayer needs to be incarnational.

Many years ago in Ingmar Bergman's movie *The Serpent's Egg* there was a scene that powerfully illustrated incarnational love. It ran along these lines: A priest has just finished presiding at the Eucharist and is in the sacristy taking off his vestments when a woman enters. Middle-aged, needy, lonely in her marriage, and suffering terribly, she begins to sob and protest that she is unlovable: "I'm so alone, Father, nobody loves me! God is so far away! I don't think He could love me anyway. Not the way I am! Everything is so dark for me!" At first, the priest is more irritated than compassionate, but at one point he says to the woman: "Kneel down and I will bless you. God seems far away. He cannot touch you right now, I know that, but I am going to put my hands on your head. I will touch you and pray for you to let you know that you are not alone, not unlovable, not in the darkness. God is here and God does love you. When I touch you, God will touch you." This is someone who is praying as a true Christian, someone who is giving *incarnational* skin and bones to his prayer.

Christ incarnates Himself in us, the members of His Body, that we may reach out to others incarnationally.

Paul Evdokimov said about incarnational prayer:

> *It is not enough to say prayers; one must become, be prayer, prayer incarnate. It is not enough to have moments of praise. All of life, each act, every gesture, even the smile of the human face, must become a hymn of adoration, an offering, a prayer. One should offer not what one has, but what one is.* *

THE BODY IS VIVIFIED BY THE HOLY SPIRIT

Just as my own body is made up of millions of cells— all vivified by one soul, governed by one head, and presided over by one mind—so, too, all of us who have been incorporated into Christ through Baptism, Chrismation and the Eucharist are cells in the one Body of Christ. We are one, because we are vivified by one soul, Who is the Holy Spirit; we are presided over by one indi-

* *The Sacrament of Love*. Paul Evdokimov. SVS Press. Crestwood, N.Y. 1985.

visible head, Christ Jesus Who is the Head of the Body. "What the soul is to the body, the Holy Spirit is to the Church," said Blessed Augustine. Permeated by grace and glory, we become, according to the Scripture,

1. the people of God,
2. the body of Christ,
3. temples of the Holy Spirit.

The word church never means a building anywhere in the Bible. If you said to an early Christian, "What a beautiful church" as you pointed to a building, he would not know what you were talking about. *Church* meant not a building but the body of Christ, the people of God.

HOW WILL GOD DO IT WITHOUT YOU?

So we ask, is there some wrong somewhere that must be made right? How will God do it without you? Is there some fear to be allayed in a troubled heart? How will God allay that fear without you? Is there someone who needs to be guided to a higher road? How will God lead him there without you? Is there some home shattered by hatred that needs the love of Christ? How will Christ bring that love there except through you? Toward the very end of the New Testament, we read that "God will wipe away all tears from their eyes." That He will do, but He needs to use your words and your compassion and the gentle touch of your hand to do it. Christ needs you. He needs me! He needs all of us. Today we Christians make up the only body through which Christ can act to make real His love and peace to the world. C.S. Lewis wrote, "God seems to do nothing of Himself which He can possibly delegate to His creatures."

A faithful young Christian lad who was left without food and shoes after a disaster was told by an unbeliever, "If God loved you, would not He send you food and shoes?" The boy replied, "God did tell someone, but that 'someone' forgot." How often have *we* forgotten?

The church, then, has on it the marks of its Lord—the divine become human, the Word made flesh. On the one hand, the Church is a divine organism, owing its origin to God, indwelt by the Holy Spirit, and ruled by Christ, the only Head. On the other hand, it is thoroughly human, incarnated in thousands of congregations, committees, financial statements, fair-share pledges and parish councils—all the necessary machinery of human activity. Thus, like Christ, the Church is a divinely established body, *koinonia*, that is both human and divine.

THREE ASPECTS OF THE BODY OF CHRIST

Instead of defining the Church formally, the Bible uses a great variety of figures of speech and poetic images to describe it. The Church is the *building* of which Christ is the foundation. The Church is the *Bride* of whom Christ is the Bridegroom.

St. Chrysostom describes the body of Christ as follows,

He [Christ] brings us into unity by means of many images.... He is the Head, we are the body; ... He

*is the Foundation, we the building; He the Vine, we
the branches; He the Bridegroom, we the bride; He
the Shepherd, we the sheep; He is the Way, we they
who walk therein;*

*Again, we are the temple, He the Indweller
(enoikos); He the First-begotten, we the brothers;
He the Heir, we the co-heirs; He the Life, we the
living; He the Resurrection, we those who rise; He
the Light, we the illuminated. All these things indi-
cate unity; and they allow no void interval, not
even the smallest.*

The Church is also the body whose Head is Christ.
"You are the Body of Christ and individually members of
it" (1 Cor. 12:27). We can read this verse in three different ways.

First, we can place the emphasis on Christ: "You are
the Body of CHRIST." In other words, the Church is not
a society that we created. It owes its existence to the life,
death and resurrection of its founder, not to any human
design. The Church can never be true to its nature if it
merely reflects the views of those who happen to be its
members or its official leaders. It is really the Church,
only as it represents Christ and speaks "the mind of
Christ". It fails to be the Church, if it proclaims only what
people like to hear. "You are the body of CHRIST."

"YOU ARE THE BODY OF CHRIST"

Secondly, we can place the emphasis on the word YOU. "YOU are the Body of Christ." In Corinth the witness to Christ depended not on Paul, not on some single leader, but on the Corinthian Christians as a body. Yet who were the Corinthian Christians? They were very ordinary Christians with so many shortcomings and failures that St. Paul takes up a large part of his two letters to reprimand them for their sins. Yet he insists that it is they who represent the exalted Christ in a city where sexual license was glorified. In the midst of such a sinful city, it was through this little group of inconsequential people that Corinth was to come to know what Christ meant for its life. "YOU are the Body of Christ."

"WE ARE ALL CREW"

Leslie Newbigin tells us that in India the newly baptized were trained to communicate their faith immediately after baptism to non-Christians. Upon being baptized, they were sent to a neighboring village to communicate to their pagan neighbors what they had learned in catechism and to present them for baptism.[*] Marshall McLuhan said once, "There are no passengers on spaceship earth. We are all crew." This is especially true of the Church as the body of Christ. The supreme glory of the Christian is that he/she is part of the body of Christ on earth. It is not just the priest who is ordained to do the work of evangelism,

[*] *The Good Shepherd.* Wm. B. Eerdmans Publ. Co. Grand Rapids, MI 1977.

of spreading the Good News of Jesus. Every Orthodox lay person is ordained into the priesthood of believers through the Sacrament of Chrismation. The role of the parish council is not just to look after the secular "business" matters of the parish, but to promote with the bishop and the priest the total spiritual mission of the Church as the body of Christ. "*You* are the body of Christ."

We often hear people say, "The church should do something about this." We forget that *we* are the church.

BODY: NOT INDIVIDUAL UNITS

Thirdly, we can place the emphasis on the word BODY: "You are the BODY of Christ", not just a collection of individual units, each standing alone, but a BODY; all members being knit and tied together in a common bond to Christ. How well this BODY emphasis is expressed in Orthodox liturgy and iconography! The walls of the church are covered with saints to make us feel that when we come to church to pray, we come as members of God's family, a body. The family located in heaven and the family located on earth in the local parish—all pray and work together as the one body of our Lord. We do not pray alone; we pray *together*, as a family, as a body, to our Lord. Infallibility resides not in any individual single member (such as the Pope or the Patriarch) but in the entire BODY, the Church, which the Holy Spirit guides to the fullness of truth. The decisions of an Ecumenical Council are made by bishops but they are recognized as infallible only after the total Church, clergy and laity, ratifies and accepts them. The Orthodox Church is hierarchical but it is also conciliar; it is not just hierarchical. It consists of laypeople, clergy and bishops—not just laypeople and not just priests, and not just bishops, but *all together* constituting one body that is guided, animated and vivified by the Holy Spirit.

THE *SOBORNOST* PRINCIPLE

Alexis Khomiakov quoted with approval the Encyclical of the Eastern Patriarchs (1848) wherein they stated that in the Orthodox Church infallibility of doctrine resides not in a Pope but "solely in the *ecumenicity* of the Church bound together by mutual love." Such infallibility (correctness) of teaching is "entrusted not to the care of one hierarchy but of all the people of the Church, who are the Body of Christ".*

Khomiakov's view of the Church as an organic community of love had a profound influence on the subsequent development of Russian Orthodox ecclesiology and shaped the meaning of the term *sobornost* which became a central concept for Orthodox ecclesiology. *Sobornost* is a term that may be translated as "togetherness" or "collegiality". It is a term that expresses the Eastern Orthodox emphasis on conciliarity over against the Roman Catholic teaching of papal infallibility and the Protestant tendency toward individualism.

Fr. Thomas Hopko summarized this clearly when he wrote,

---

* *Ultimate Questions: An Anthology of Modern Russian Religious Thought.* Alexander Schmemann. Holt, Rinehart and Winston. N.Y. 1965.

*Most important for us to see today, and to under-
stand clearly, is that the Church of God and Christ
is the whole pleroma of the faithful, not just the
ordained clergy. God's people and Christ's Body
and the Holy Spirit's temple, theologically, spiritually, and canonically, always denotes the Church
as a whole, never only the small number of the
baptized who are ordained as bishops, presbyters,
and deacons for service to the whole body of baptized believers.* *

PROSKOMIDI: AN ICON OF THE BODY OF CHRIST

During the service of the *Proskomidi* the priest pre-
pares the bread and the wine for the holy Eucharist. The
manner in which this is done presents us with a beautiful
icon of the Church as the body of Christ.

First, the priest takes the bread presented for the
Eucharist, cuts out and places on the paten a pyramid
piece, called "the Lamb", which will later be consecrated
for the Eucharist. Then he cuts a triangular cube of bread
and places it to the right of the Lamb, commemorating the
Mother of God.

On the left side of the Lamb, he continues to recreate
the Church out of small particles of bread. He begins with
John the Baptist. Then he cuts particles of bread for the
Old Testament prophets, the apostles, the holy hierarchs,
the martyrs, beginning with St. Stephen; then our God-

* *Speaking the Truth in Love*. Thomas Hopko. SVS Press. Crestwood, N.Y.
2004.

bearing Fathers and Mothers, the Holy Unmercenary Physicians, Cosmas and Damian, Panteleimon, and others; then the ancestors of God, Joachim and Anna, together with other saints. Finally, he remembers with the ninth particle of bread the saint whose liturgy is being celebrated, either St. John Chrysostom, St. Basil the Great, or St. James. Thus, the priest has created on the left side of Christ, nine categories of saints, from the history of the church.

Below these, the priest proceeds to remove particles of bread for the living and the dead (whose names were submitted for prayer by congregants). Thus, around the Lamb of God is gathered the entire Church, the entire Body of Christ, from the Old Testament through the New Testament and the early history of the Church down to the present, both living and departed. This whole recreation of the Church as the body of Christ, gathered around the Lamb, is in effect an icon of the Church. This is then carried in procession through the church at the Great Entrance and placed on the holy table. And when the Lamb is consecrated for the Eucharist during the Liturgy, it is the Lamb surrounded by the entire church, the whole body of Christ, the church militant and the church triumphant. The *epiclesis* prayer at the moment of consecration prays for the descent of the Holy Spirit not only for the consecration of the Lamb, but also upon all those present in the liturgy so that they, like the Gifts, might manifest the real Presence of Christ in the world. It is at that point that we experience Pentecost and are filled with the Spirit. Since we ourselves are present on the paten just below the Lamb in the particles of bread that represent us, we too are consecrated through the Holy Spirit to become the body of Christ, the temple of the Holy Spirit, and the people of God. When we receive the Eucharist, we indeed become the living body of Christ since Christ Himself comes to abide in us. That is why we say that we do not merely go to church, we are the church, the body of Christ, wherever we go.

Following the reception of the Eucharist, the priest places all the particles of bread that are left on the paten into the chalice with a prayer for the "washing away by your holy blood of the sins of your servants here remembered." We are indeed "washed by the blood of the Lamb" which takes away the sins of the world.

Thus in every liturgy the body of Christ is re-constituted and empowered by the indwelling of the Spirit and the Eucharist to be what it is, the body through which Christ together with the Father and the Holy Spirit are present and active in the world today.

PHYLETISM AND THE BODY OF CHRIST

It must be lamented that the teaching of the Church as the body of Christ is seriously jeopardized, if not denied, by the heresy of phyletism, which was condemned by the Ecumenical Patriarchate in 1872, but which continues to divide the Orthodox Church today. Phyletism (nationalism) is a euphemistic word for *raw tribalism*. Through a multiplicity of bishops in the same city, for example, the Orthodox in the U.S. especially, have crystalized an ecclesiology tainted by tribalism. Ethnic separation has become the curse of Orthodoxy. How can we say that we are the one body of Christ when church and national identity are confused to such a degree that in New York City alone a few years ago there were nineteen different Orthodox bishops belonging to nineteen different national jurisdictions, whose faith was identical in all points; the only thing that separated them was their national identity! Orthodox canon law dictates emphatically that there should be only one bishop in each city.   Religious nationalism (phyletism) has shown itself to be what someone aptly called a "modern form of idolatry". Such tribalism destroys the unity of the body of Christ. It needs to be transformed into a community (*koinonia*). The body of Christ supersedes all national identities. It is Catholic, not Greek or Russian or Serbian. As we confess in the Nicene Creed, we believe in "one, holy, catholic, and apostolic church".

INDIVIDUALISM AND THE BODY OF CHRIST

Another enemy of the unity of the body of Christ is individualism. Christos Yannaras describes how such individualism destroys the *koinonia* or communion that should exist in the body of Christ. He writes,

A parish contains thousands of people, often tens of thousands, and there is no personal communion or sense of being a body. People do not gather in the churches to constitute the body of the Church, to manifest and realize the true life of the communion of persons; they come to satisfy their individual religious needs and to pray as individuals…more

*alone perhaps than on the sportsground or at the
cinema.* *

Individualism is something that prevents the Church
from being the body of Christ. Dr. Nicholas Afanasiev,
noted Orthodox liturgical scholar, commented on the individualism that he saw prevalent when people came to
receive the Body and Blood of Jesus, the sacrament that
transforms all of us into the One Body of Christ:

> *Each one remains a separate atom in relation to
> all the others whom we do not even know. Often,
> we do not know those with whom we approach the
> chalice. We enter the church building for ourselves
> alone, and not in order to "gather together as
> church".*

Such individualism separates one from the body. And
we know that an individual cell cannot live outside the
body; it dies. "One Christian is no Christian," said
Tertullian. There is no such thing as a solitary Christian.

Life is not a one-man show. We are members of a
body. Through sin we may cut ourselves off from the
body, from the One Who is the very source of our being.
But Christ is constantly inviting us to reconnect, to restore
our connection to Him and His body through repentance.

Our purpose as members of the body of Christ is to be
servants of God and of one another—of "the least of the
brethren" to the glory of God the Father, the Son and the

* *The Freedom of Morality.* Christos Yannaras. SVS Press. Crestwood, N.Y.
1996.

Holy Spirit. The greatest schism, said Oliver Clement, is the schism between the sacrament of the altar and the sacrament of the brother/sister. The same Christ Who meets us at the altar in the Sacrament of the Eucharist meets us everyday in the sacrament of "the least of the brethren" (Matt. 25). The schism, separation, is caused by our not recognizing and ignoring Jesus when He comes to us disguised as a refugee or prisoner.

CHRIST RENDERS THE BODY HOLY AND WITHOUT BLEMISH

In Ephesians 5:23-32, St. Paul describes the relationship between Christ and His body, the Church. He says that, "Christ is the head of the church…(he) loved the church and gave Himself for her that He might sanctify and cleanse her with the washing of water by the word that He might present her to Himself a glorious church, not having spot or wrinkle or any such thing, but that she should be holy and without blemish … (the Lord) nourishes and cherishes the church … we are members of His body, of His flesh, and of His bones." St. Paul is saying here that Christ loves the Church; He gives Himself up for her; He makes her holy; without a single mark of imperfection; He nourishes and cherishes her.

HOW CAN THE BODY OF CHRIST BE HOLY?

But what does St. Paul mean when he says that the Church is "…a glorious church, not having spot or wrinkle or any such thing, but that she should be holy and without blemish"? (Eph. 5:27) How can the Church be "holy and without blemish" when *we* the members of the body of Christ, are not holy? All of us are sinners—bishops, priests, deacons, lay people—not one of us is without sin. How can the Church be holy when we, her members, are anything but holy?

The Church teaches that the sins of the members of the Body do not affect the essential sinless nature of the Church as described by St. Paul (Eph. 5:27). The Orthodox delegates to the Evanston Assembly of the WCC (1954) explained this clearly when they stated:

> *The Church's holiness is not vitiated (spoiled) by the sins and failures of her members. They cannot in any way lessen or exhaust the inexhaustible holiness of the divine life which from the head of the Church (Christ) is diffused throughout all the body.*

The Church (Body of Christ) is holy and remains holy not because of us, but because it is the body of the All-holy and sinless Christ.

Dr. Peter Bouteneff, an Orthodox theologian, explains what happens when the members of the body of Christ (Church) sin:

> *There ought to be no pretence that, because the Church itself is a sinless body, its members are sinless. The holy Church is not a community of the sinless, but precisely the hospital of the sinner. As sinners, as those who constantly and repetitively miss the mark of holiness, who ever fall short of*

our great vocation as human beings made in God's image, as people who do damage to ourselves, each other, and the world, we need healing. The Church, the holy and spotless body of Christ, is the place of healing for the sinners who constitute its membership.

Therefore, there is a certain irony built into the Church, given its nature and function, and its members. This irony is worked out in a kind of double-functionality of the church: it is the hospital for the sick, but it remains the body of Christ. The point is that its holiness and sinlessness as a body serves not only to heal the sinner, but also ever to call the sinner to holiness. Indeed, it could not be an effective healing place for sinners were it not itself holy and sinless....

(When we sin) ... we fail to be the Church.

Every personal and corporate failure or falling-away calls for a personal and corporate return. And life in the Church consists in a constant cycle of falling away and coming back. In the sacrament of penance, we reflect on how we live our life, we bring it before God with the aim not only of personal healing but also of being reconciled with the Church, of again becoming the Church. And in this sacrament, the minister and penitent pray together precisely for this reconciliation: "re-unite him/her to your holy flock".

So when a member of the holy Church sins, he or she in effect falls away from the Church's calling, and must strive to be reunited to it. The gift of the church's holiness is also a calling, and that calling is ever before us as a measure. We are to take that calling with utter seriousness, and repent at our failures to live up to it.

At the same time, it is useful to note certain things that do not happen when members of the Church sin.

When we fall and seek to be reunited to the Church, we seek to re-become the Church. It is not the Church that falls—the Church is raising the fallen, calling back the sinner to itself. Therefore, while the sin of any church member pollutes the community, and while entire communities are liable to sin, that sin does not taint the essential nature of the Church, for the Church is more than the community of its members. *

The Church is indeed something more than the sum total of its members. It is the body of Christ.

Thus, as Dr. Bouteneff goes on to say, "Whenever the Church is not being actively missionary, preaching, and teaching and being socially responsible—ministering to and advocating for the poor, sick and oppressed, struggling

---

* *Beyond the East/West Divide.* Anna Marie Aagard and Peter Bouteneff. WCC Publications. Geneva, Switzerland. 2001

34

for justice—it is failing to be the Church." Here is where each one of us needs to examine one's self carefully by asking probing questions such as: How often and in how many ways have I failed to be the Church to my spouse, to my children, to my neighbor? I am a member of the body of Christ, but does my life reflect Jesus the Light of the World? How often have I failed to be the Church? Do I need to re-become a member of the body through repentance? Do I need to be reminded that the Lord baptized and ordained me as a member of His body through Holy Chrismation to serve as "salt, yeast and light" in the world? How often do we need to be reminded of Mother Maria's famous words:

> *At the Last Judgment I will not be asked whether I satisfactorily practiced asceticism, nor how many prostrations and bows I have made before the holy table. I will be asked whether I fed the hungry, clothed the naked, visited the sick and the prisoner in jail. That is all I will be asked.*

"You are the body of Christ and individually members of it" (1 Cor. 12:27).

CHRIST IS THE HEAD

On the long high front wall of a church that was just being completed, an artist started painting a picture of Christ as the Good Shepherd. Only the firm brush strokes outlining the head of Christ with shepherd's staff could be seen. A stranger stopped in and asked curiously, "When will the picture be finished?" A workman replied, "That picture? It is finished."

"Finished?" repeated the startled visitor. "Why all it is, is the outline of a head with a staff. Most of it is still missing—the eyes, mouth, arms, legs and feet—the whole body is missing!"

"You won't see that on a wall," the workman replied. "The body of Christ is the congregation of people who will be worshipping in this church. The body of Christ is the Church."

St. Paul writes, "He (Christ) is the head of the body, the Church" (Col. 1:18). "He (God) has put all things under His feet and has made Him (Christ) the head over all things for the Church, which is His body, the fullness of Him Who fills all in all" (Eph. 1:22-23).

St. Chrysostom said once, "Christ is the head of the body, but what can the head do without hands, without feet, without eyes, without ears, without a mouth?" The Church is the completion of Christ. So great is Christ's love for the Church that He considers Himself incomplete, as it were, if He does not have united to Him as His Body, the Church, i.e., you and me!

Of course, we must realize here that the analogy is not completely true. In the human anatomy the head cannot exist without the body. But Christ as the Eternal Son of God has existed from all eternity without the Church as His body.

God without man is still God. Man without God is nothing. Although this is true, what Augustine said is also true: "Without God, we cannot. Without us, God will not." Why? Because God has chosen to work through

His body, the Church, i.e., through us.

Dr. Peter Bouteneff explains this teaching as follows:

Christ is the head of the body (Eph. 5:23). The body and the head are of course intimately linked but, further, they have a certain mutual dependence on one another. There is no body without a head, but neither is there a head without a body. As St. Paul puts it, neither can say to the other, "I have no need of you" (1 Cor. 12:21).

If we take these meanings to their full extent, then to call the Church the body of Christ, with Christ as the head of the body, means not only that the Church is headed by Christ and utterly needs Christ, but also that the Church somehow completes Christ. Or, as Bishop Kallistos (Ware) writes, "The Church is the extension of the incarnation, the place where the incarnation perpetuates itself."*

"CHRIST IS LIVING IN THESE TEN FINGERS"

A practical expression of this truth is the testimony of a medical missionary, a physician. After a seven-hour operation, he said, "I get the wonderful feeling that for seven hours Christ is living in these ten fingers! I have the priceless awareness that these hands become the hands of Jesus bringing healing to one of His children." He was

* *Beyond the East/West Divide.* Anna Marie Aagard and Peter Bouteneff. WCC Publications. Geneva, Switzerland. 2001

right! Those hands were indeed the hands of the Master Surgeon, Jesus Christ.

St. John Chrysostom said, "The Church is the complement of Christ in the same manner in which the head completes the body and the body is completed by the head. He has prepared the whole race in common to follow Him, to cling to Him, to accompany His train. Observe how St. Paul introduces God as having need of all the members. This means that only then will the head be filled up, when the body is rendered perfect, when we are all together, co-united and knit together with Him."

As the Head of the body, Christ controls and gives orders to the various members. He is the brain; the One in Whom all the fullness of God dwells bodily. "He is the image of the invisible God, the first-born of all creation; for in him all things were created…. He is before all things, and in him all things hold together. He is the head of the body, the Church…" (Col. 1:15-18).

What a privilege God bestows on us when He ties us so intimately with Christ and with each other as to make us constitute one body—one *koinonia*—with Him as the Head. When we meditate on this analogy, we come to look at prayer as the members of the body (the Church) reporting for duty to the Head, the Commander-in-Chief of the Universe. As Isaiah said, "Here I am, Lord. Send me." Not as one wag put it, "Here I am, Lord. I'll think it over." Or, "Here I am Lord. Send him." But, "Here I am. Send *me*."

C.S. Lewis, the great Christian apologist, emphasized the important role each member of the body of Christ plays in God's plan of saving the world:

We do know that no man can be saved except through Christ; we don't know that only those who know Him can be saved through Him. But in the meantime, if you're worried about the people outside, the most unreasonable thing you can do is to remain outside yourself. Christians are Christ's body, the organism through which He works. Every addition to that body enables Him to do more. If you want to help those outside you must add your own little cell to the body of Christ who can help them. Cutting off a man's fingers would be an odd way of getting him to do more work.

A VARIETY OF GIFTS IN THE BODY

St. Basil realizes that there are in the Church, as the body of Christ, a variety of gifts, all given by the same Spirit, and a variety of services all under the direction of the same Lord. "Now you are the body of Christ and individually members of it. And God has appointed in the Church first apostles, second prophets, third teachers,…then healers, helpers, administrators…Are all apostles? Are all prophets? Are all teachers?…" (1 Cor. 12:4-11; 27-29). Elsewhere St. Paul writes, "For as in one body we have many members, and all the members do not have the same function, so we, though many, are one body in Christ, and individually members one of another. Having gifts that differ according to the grace given to us, let us use them: if prophecy, in proportion to our faith; if service, in our serving; he who teaches, in his teaching…he who contributes, in liberality; he who gives aid, with zeal; he who does acts of mercy, with cheerfulness" (Rom. 5:4-8).

Just as in the body there are many parts, many organs, so in the body of Christ there are varieties of gifts, says Paul. As in the body the various members work together to contribute to the health and wholeness of the body, so in that other body, the Church, the varieties of gifts given by the Holy Spirit are to serve "for the equipment of the saints, for the work of ministry, for building up the body of Christ, until we all attain to the unity of the faith and of the knowledge of the Son of God, to mature manhood, to the measure of the stature of the fullness of Christ" (Eph. 4:12-13).

Francis de Sales, a Western saint, described the great variety of gifts in the body magnificently when he wrote,

Our spiritual makeup is as varied as our physical. Each person has distinct gifts. Our diversity is infinite. "The sun has one kind of splendor, the moon another, and the stars another; and star differs from star in splendor" (1 Cor. 15:41). So it is with people. God's grace comes in infinite variety.

It is not helpful to ask why one person is blessed in a particular way. God's "grace is sufficient" (2 Cor. 12:9) for each one of us. Why are melons bigger than strawberries? Why do lilies grow taller than violets? Why is the rosemary not a rose or the dianthus not a marigold? Why is a peacock more glamorous than a bat? Why is a fig sweet while a lemon is acidic? These are absurd questions. The beauty of the world depends upon variety. Differences and what appear to be inequalities are essential and inescapable. This thing is not that thing.

It is the same way in the spiritual dimension. Each of us has a particular "gift from God; one has this gift, another that" (1 Cor. 7:7). It is disrespectful to ask why St. Paul and St. Peter did not have similar gifts and abilities. The church is a garden with a great variety of plants. Each one has its value and charm. It is the combination of their colors and textures that make the garden a thing of beauty.*

Father Jordan Bajis explains how each person in the Church has a uniquely different gift that is necessary for the Body to function, "…the Church needs *each* member. He has neither given all His gifts to one, nor has He given the same one gift to each; He has given a *variety* of gifts to *many*. This teaches us that every member of the body is not only *different* from other members, but that each *needs* the other's uniqueness in order to be complete."**

* *Living Love.* Francis de Sales. Edited by Bernard Bangley. Paraclete Press. 2002.
** *Common Ground.* Jordan Bajis. Light and Life Publ. Co. Mpls. MN 1989.

THE CARPENTER'S TOOLS

There is a fable about a conversation that took place in a carpenter's shop. Brother Hammer was in his chair. The meeting had informed him that he must leave because he is much too noisy. But he said, "If I am to leave this carpenter's shop, Brother Pencil must also go. He is so insignificant that he makes very little impression."

Little Brother Pencil arose and said, "All right, but if I go, Brother Screw must also go. You have to turn him around and around, again and again, to ever get him anywhere."

And Brother Screw said, "If you wish, I will go, but Brother Plane must leave also. All his work is on the surface. There is no depth to him."

And to this, Brother Plane replied, "Well, if I go, Brother Ruler will have to go, for he is always measuring other people as if he is the only one who is ever right."

Brother Ruler then complained against Brother Sandpaper and said, "I just don't care. But if I go, Brother Sandpaper has to go too. He is too rough and he's always rubbing people the wrong way."

And in the midst of this discussion the Carpenter of Nazareth walked in. He put on his apron and went to his bench to make a table. He used the screw, the pencil, the ruler, the sandpaper, the saw, the hammer, the plane, and all the other tools.

And after the day's work was over and the table was finished, Brother Saw arose and said, "Brethren, I perceive that all of us are laborers together."

There was no accusation against one of these tools that

was not absolutely true. And yet the Carpenter of Nazareth used every one of them. And there was not a place where he used any one of them where another one could have been used.

The Carpenter of Nazareth is building His Church—and He needs all of us working together to do the job. No one can say that some other member of the body of Christ is not needed. We are all uniquely important in working for the Master. He needs and uses each one of us with our unique, God-given gifts. "You are the body of Christ and individually members of it" (1 Cor. 12:27).

THE CHURCH IS NOT A SOLO
BUT A SYMPHONY

The Church is not a *solo* but a *symphony* of many members with many gifts taking orders from the One Leader (Christ) and working together to produce something beautiful, a symphony of love, justice, joy and peace for God's glory.

Christians should never make a great to-do about serving the Lord. He has given each one of us our own gift for the purpose of serving. Does the hand boast when it carries out the will of the heart?

Bishop Kallistos Ware wrote, "The Holy Spirit is a Spirit of freedom. While Christ unites us, the Holy Spirit ensures infinite variety in the Church: at Pentecost the tongues of fire were 'cloven' or divided, descending *separately* upon each of those present. The gift of the Spirit is a gift to the Church, but it is at the same time a personal gift, appropriated by each in his own way. 'There are diversities of gifts, but the same Spirit' (1 Cor. 12:4). Life in the Church does not mean the ironing out of human variety, nor the imposition of a rigid and uniform pattern upon all alike, but the exact opposite. The saints, so far from displaying a drab monotony, have developed the most vivid and distinctive personalities. It is not holiness but evil which is dull".

DIFFERENT STOREHOUSES FOR DIFFERENT CROPS

As I was driving through the countryside one day, I noticed the many kinds of storage sheds used for crops. Long warehouses, built into the cool earth, store potatoes; tall warehouses store grain; round silos store silage; open barns on poles store hay. Each is designed with a different shape to do a different job.

Aren't we all storehouses of God's gifts? God designed each one of us for a specific job. Just as the storehouses for crops are not alike, neither are we. We have different talents and abilities stored within us, all to be used for God's glory.

There is an infinite and delightful variety of gifts in the body of Christ. Someone said once, "I've learned that you cannot play a symphony on a piccolo. I have been trying to do so all along. Next Sunday, I am going to speak to the priest about joining the body of Christ, the Church. I want to play my small part in God's great orchestra."

A DISEMBODIED VIEW OF THE
CHRISTIAN FAITH

The Church is an orchestra, a body—the body of Christ. Like the piccolo player, some Christians believe that as long as one has a personal relationship with Jesus, one doesn't need to belong to the Church. For such a person the Christian life is viewed as an individualistic journey where the body—the community of faith—is of secondary importance. It is the person's personal relationship with Jesus that makes him a Christian. It is a Lone Ranger type of Christianity. According to this Jesus-and-me mentality, the individual decides what God's truth is, apart from the body. This is a disembodied view of the Christian faith that ties in with the individualistic ethos of western culture which views churches as societies of like-minded individuals who choose to organize in order to pursue their subjective personal tasks. But the Church is not such a social club. It is the very body of Christ into which we were grafted through holy baptism. Such a belief in the body of Christ is diametrically opposed to the individualism of western culture. We must realize that Orthodoxy does not consider the Church as a mere human organization, or as a voluntary association of individuals that is irrelevant to our salvation. To participate in the Church is to be in the Kingdom of God here and now; it is to be in communion with the Holy Trinity. Far from being a sociological construct, the Church is a sacrament, a sign of God's mysterious presence in the world.

"The eye cannot say to the hand, 'I don't need you!' And the hand cannot say to the feet, 'I don't need you!'"

One part of the body cannot live without all the other parts. A person may say, "I can have a relationship with God without going to church." But that's not what God says. God says that if you are a Christian at all, it's only because you are part of the body of Christ. No part of the body can go on living without being connected to the rest of the body.

THE CHURCH AS THE VISIBLE BODY OF CHRIST

The Orthodox Church stresses the importance of membership in a particular visible Christian community—the body of Christ. Many who never darken the door of a church call themselves Christians. They claim to belong to the "invisible" church. Orthodox Christianity believes, not in an invisible, but in a wholly visible Church which is the body of Christ in the world today. Grafted into this body through baptism, we are constantly nourished with Christ through the umbilical cord of the Eucharist. After all, it was Jesus Himself Who said, "Unless you eat my flesh and drink my blood you have no life in you" (John 6:53). One cannot receive the Eucharist if one lives apart from the Church. One cannot be a Christian alone. This is what the expression "Outside the Church there is no salvation" means. God established the Church, His body, and He has chosen to abide in the Church and work through the Church to accomplish His work in the world today.

The answer to the question, "Are you saved?" is "Yes, I am among the people whom God is saving." The Church is the arena in which God is "working out (our) salvation" (Phil. 2:12-13). To consider yourself a Christian merely by a personal relationship with Jesus, not needing the Church, is to introduce a dangerous individualism in the Church. Christianity is not a solo but a symphony. A personal relationship with Jesus does not grow on trees. It is a relationship that grows and flourishes as long as we remain attached to Christ as living members of His body, the Church.

For Fr. Georges Florovsky, the Church was never simply a society of like-minded individuals but a community, a divinely established living organism of love and truth,

> *Christianity from the very beginning existed as a corporate reality, as a community. To be Christian meant just to belong to the community. Nobody could be Christian by himself, as an isolated individual, but only together with the brethren, in a "togetherness" with them ... Christianity means a "common life", a life in common.**

Radical individualism is an American phenomenon. It is an individualism that says, "I don't need the church. It's just Jesus and me. I decide what the Bible teaches, etc." This is not what Jesus taught and not what the early church believed. This type of Jesus-and-me individualism is the opposite of *koinonia*. The early Christians said, "It seemed good to the Holy Spirit and to *us....*" (Acts 15:28). They did not say, "It seemed good to the Holy Spirit and to *me....*"

* *Bible, Church, Tradition: An Eastern Orthodox View*. Nordland Publ. Co. Belmont, MA.

We were baptized into a body. When the Holy Spirit appeared on Pentecost, He descended not on just one apostle but on all of them together as a body. It is in the body of Christ that we have the opportunity to develop a lasting personal relationship with Christ. It is in the body that we grow into the stature and fullness of Christ.

THE BODY IS INDWELT BY THE HOLY SPIRIT

It is significant to remember that Christ began His public ministry immediately following His baptism in the River Jordan when he was anointed by the Holy Spirit. As the Holy Spirit animated and vivified the ministry of Jesus, so the same Holy Spirit came on Pentecost to abide in and empower the mystical body of Christ, the Church. Dr. Peter Bouteneff explains,

... the Church is a body in which the Holy Spirit of God dwells, in all his fullness. To begin with, the same spirit that anoints Christ, that fills Christ, and through which we recognize Jesus as the Christ, is the Spirit that fills and anoints Christ's Body, the Church. Moreover, we look to the descent of the Spirit at Pentecost as the particular inauguration of this indwelling of the Spirit in the Church, an indwelling of the Spirit to the fullest extent.

What is meant by this "fullness"? It would seem absurd to quantify the Holy Spirit and his activity, to say that the Spirit is "more here than there".

And yet, while we know that the Holy Spirit "blows where it will" (John 3:8), the Spirit also descends in a specific and concrete way upon the disciples at Pentecost. The Church is the continuation of that community which received the Holy Spirit in this direct and particular way, and continues to be indwelt by the Spirit in his fullness. The Church, "which is [Christ's] body, the fullness of him who fills all in all" (Eph. 1:23), indwelt by the Holy Spirit, participates fully in the perfection, the unity, the sanctity and holiness, the completeness and universality, and missionary character of Christ and the Holy Spirit.*

When asked, "Why should Christians today care about what the Church Fathers had to say?", Christopher Hall replied, "The Holy Spirit has a history. The church does not thrive in the first century, fail in the second, then revive in the sixteenth. The Spirit never deserts the church."**   The same Holy Spirit Who has a history, also has a body, the Church, which "continues to be indwelt by the Spirit in His fullness."

---

* *Beyond the East/West Divide*. Anna Marie Aagard and Peter Bouteneff. WCC Publications. Geneva. 2001.
** *The Habits of Highly Effective Bible Readers: A Conversation With Christopher A. Hall*. Christian History, No. 80 (2003).

THE DIVINE HUMANITY OF THE BODY OF CHRIST AS EXPRESSED BY THE THEOTOKOS

The Church has been called by some Orthodox theologians "the Divine humanity" of Christ. As the Body of Christ, the Church is both human and divine. It represents our human nature indwelt by the Lord Jesus; it represents human nature restored and transfigured by the indwelling of the Trinity. This is expressed in many icons of the Theotokos where she is pictured as holding the Christ Child, especially the *Eleousa* icon and the *Glykofilousa* (Sweet-Kissing) icons. In these icons the Theotokos represents our humanity, our human nature. She is one of us. She is the human side of the Church. Yet enthroned in her bosom is Jesus, the Son of God, Who together with the Father and the Holy Spirit, abide in her humanity, as well as in ours. Thus the Theotokos became the first member of the body of Christ, the Church. The Son of God, as well as the Holy Spirit, descended upon her at the Annunciation and remained with her. It is for this reason that she is often pictured together with the Christ Child as the *Platytera* on the front wall of many Orthodox Churches. She is the first Christian, the first member of the body of Christ, the Church. She leads us in our prayers to her Son who is depicted in the dome as the Pantocrator. Holding Jesus in her left hand, she points to Him with the elongated fingers of her right hand, inviting us to accept Him as "the Way, the Truth and the Life". Jesus, in turn, expresses His love for His mother, who represents us in an extraordinary manner as described by Rowan Williams. Remember that in his tender love for the Theotokos, Jesus is expressing His love for all of us, since she is one of us. Here is Williams' very insightful description of Jesus in the *Eleousa* icon:

If we begin, as most of us tend to, with a notion that God stands at a distance waiting for us to make a move in his direction, this image should give us something of a shock. The Lord here does not wait, impassive, as we babble on about our shame and penitence, trying to persuade him that we are worth forgiving. His love is instead that of an eager and rather boisterous child, scrambling up on his mother's lap, seizing handfuls of her clothing and nuzzling his face against hers, with that extraordinary hunger for sheer physical close-ness that children will show with loving parents. Instead of the effort to bridge the enormous gap between here and there, between God and my sin-ful self, we have a movement—direct, intimate, overwhelming, even embarrassing—from God to us. Just as we might want to say to a child, "Calm down," as it pushes at us or grabs clothes and hair, so we can imagine Mary in this image half-embarrassed by the urgency and overexcitement of the child. Behind the stately postures of the icon, we can see something intensely, untidily human. This is a child who cannot bear to be separated from his mother. We have seen that God is not ashamed to be our God, to be identified as the one who is involved with us; here, though, it is as if he is not merely unashamed but positively shameless in his eagerness, longing to embrace and be embraced. It is not simply that God will deign not to mind our company; rather he is passionate for it. The image of God's action we are presented with here is of a hungry love. *

This marvelous icon expresses magnificently the passionate love of Jesus for the Theotokos, the first member of His body, as well as for us, the subsequent members of the body. The Theotokos, the first member of the body, represents us. Jesus, scrambling up His Mother's arms in a hungry love to possess her, represents God's passionate love for us—the members of His body.

THE UNITY OF THE BODY

"We are many, but we are one loaf, one body" (1 Cor. 10:17), wrote St. Paul. Though separated from God and from each other by sin, we are made one—one body—by the same Christ Who comes to dwell in each of us. "One loaf," says Paul. "What is the bread?" asks Chrysostom. "It is the body of Christ. And what do those who receive the Bread become? They become the body of Christ, not many bodies but one body. Just as the bread which is composed of many grains of wheat becomes one loaf, so we become united with Christ as one body, one loaf. You are not nourished by one bread and I by another. We all receive the same Bread to become the one body of Christ."

The celebrant priest in every liturgy prays a double invocation at the *epiclesis*: "Send down Your Holy Spirit

---

* *Ponder These Things. Praying with Icons of the Virgin.* Rowan Wiliams. Sheed and Ward Publ. Franklin, WI 2002.

on us and *on these gifts* here set forth." The people standing round the holy table and the gifts lying upon it are consecrated together so that each may become the body of Christ. Through the Eucharist Christ and the Holy Spirit come to dwell in us to make us one body, the body of Christ, the Church.

Thus the Eucharist makes us truly one *koinonia*, one body, the community of God's people.

This is brought out especially in the words of the *epiclesis* prayer of the Liturgy of St. Basil when the Holy Spirit is invoked not just for the consecration of the gifts but also for the *unity of the community*: "And to unite us all, as many as are partakers in the one bread and cup, one with another, in the communion of the one Holy Spirit." Thus, the Holy Spirit forms the Body of Christ through the Eucharist.

St. Chrysostom asks, "When Christ is so willing to unite us to Himself and to each other, why do we continue to want to remain separated from one another through hatred and lack of forgiveness?"

"JESUS HAS AIDS"

If the Church is the body of Christ, there are many practical ramifications of this truth for all of us. Let me share one of these ramifications with you.

Musa W. Dube, from Botswana, shocked her audience at a meeting on a mission sponsored by the World Council of Churches when she declared that Jesus has AIDS. Her logic: there are people in the *church who have AIDS; the church is the body of Christ; therefore, Jesus has AIDS. Hence her paraphrase of the judgment scene in Matthew 25: "I was sick with AIDS and you did not visit me. You did not wash my wounds, nor did you give me medicine…. I was stigmatized, isolated and rejected because of HIV/AIDS and you did not welcome me. I was hungry, thirsty and naked, completely dispossessed … and you did not give me food, water or any clothing. I was a powerless woman exposed to the high risk of infection and carrying a huge burden of care, and you did not come to my rescue. I was a dispossessed widow and an orphan and you did not meet my needs…. The Lord will say to us, 'Truly, I tell you, as long as you did not do it to one of the least of these members of my family, of my body, you did not do it to me.'"**

Thereby do we all stand condemned. Does anyone now wonder why we repeat the prayer *Kyrie Eleison* (Lord, have mercy) so often in the liturgy. Lord, be merciful to me, the sinner, for ignoring the fact that you have AIDS and I pay no attention!

Is there such a solidarity in other religions? One Islamic scholar wrote, "In partaking of Islam the Muslim acknowledges his dependence on God … and his solidarity with fellow Muslims." The solidarity in Islam is "with fellow Muslims". The difference with Christianity is that the believer is called to union with all mankind and with

* *International Review of Mission.* October 2002.

all of creation. Thus, the solidarity of Islam is not the same as the mystical union with God and all people as experienced in Orthodox Christianity.

WE NEED EACH OTHER

The many practical ramifications of the Church as the body of Christ are expressed in one of Aesop's fables called *The Stomach and the Members*. It seems that the members of the body had a meeting one day. They decided to go on strike because the stomach was getting all the food while they were doing all the work.

For a day or two the hands lay idle, so the mouth couldn't receive any food, and the teeth had no work to do. After a couple more days the hands noticed they could hardly move. The mouth was parched and dry, the legs were unable to support the rest of the body.

So the story concludes: "Even the stomach in its dull, quiet way is doing work necessary for the whole body, and all members must work together or the whole body will go to pieces."

As members of the same body, we need each other. God has created the body that there may be no discord, but that the members may care for each other. As the hand cannot say to the eye, "I have no need of you," so none of us can say to the other, "I can get along without you." St. Paul says, "Bear ye one another's burdens, and so fulfill the law of Christ" (Gal. 6:2).

NO INSIGNIFICANT MEMBERS

There are no insignificant or unimportant members in the human body. Man can grasp, manipulate, and perform various daily tasks with his hands only because of his unattractive little thumb. Try picking up anything without a thumb. Ever try balancing yourself without using your ugly little toes?

Each member of the body works for the whole body. The eye sees for the whole body. The hand labors for the whole body. The teeth chew for the whole body. The stomach digests for the whole body. So do the heart, the kidney, the liver. They all work for the whole body. Not one of them does anything in isolation but always in *koinonia*. The Lord created us to be not independent but *interdependent*. He created us to be not an assembly of self-made individuals but a communion, a body of believers dependent upon Him and each other.

Every cell in the body has its own specific job in interdependence with every other cell. The only cells which insist on being independent and autonomous are the cancer cells. Their uncontrolled growth leads to death.

St. John Chrysostom explains how the unity of the body works:

> *God has created all people spiritually equal.*
> *Every person has the same propensity for good and*
> *evil. Every person has the same choice, as to*
> *whether to obey God or to defy Him. Yet in other*
> *ways, we are very unequal. Some people are high-*
> *ly intelligent, while others have feeble intellects.*

Some people are physically strong and healthy,
while others are weak and prone to illness. Some
people are handsome and attractive, while others
are plain. Those who are gifted in some way
should not despise those less gifted. On the con-
trary, God has distributed gifts and blessings in
such a way that every person has a particular
place and purpose within a society—and thus
everyone is equally necessary for a society to func-
tion well. So do not resent the fact that someone is
more intelligent or stronger than you are. Instead
give thanks for their intelligence and strength, from
which you benefit. And then ask yourself: "What is
my gift, and thence what is my place in society?"
When you have answered this question, and you
act according to your answer, all contempt and all
resentment will melt away.

If I am a foot in the body of Christ but try to do the
work of a hand, I will not be doing what Jesus wants me
to do. The other members of the body will suffer.

SOS FOR OXYGEN: IMMEDIATE RESPONSE

When the small toe is smashed by a stone, it sends an
SOS for oxygen and red blood corpuscles to the rest of the
body. Suppose the heart would say, "I get so annoyed by
these small things. We can get along without that little
toe. I am too important to be bothered by a small toe. I
must conserve my energy." And so the small toe dies and
is amputated. And suppose this self-centered heart, a part

of the body, continues to live like this, so that one after another the members of the body die. What is the result? Why the heart dies too, of course. It cannot live by itself. When all the dependent members die, the heart loses its meaning and dies. The heart, after all, is not sufficient unto itself. By a strange paradox, it finds its meaning in being of service to the other members. Have you ever seen a heart, detached from the body, pulsating on a dish in surgery? It is a very unpleasant sight, because it is not what the heart is meant for. Yet this is an accurate picture of any member of the Church who thinks he/she can get along without the other members of the body. The church is a symphony not a solo. It is a *koinonia* of interdependent members. "In the mystery of Christ there is no such thing as an individual, only a person in relationship, in baptismal and eucharistic communion with God and other persons."*

THE SIGNIFICANCE OF DIVERSITY

Metropolitan John of Pergamon (Zizioulas) stresses the significance of diversity in the Church's life based on 1 Cor. 12. He writes,

Each member of the community is indispensable, carrying his or her gifts to the one body. All members are needed but not all are the same; they are needed precisely because they are different.

* *The Journey Into God.* Kenneth L. Bakken. Augsburg Publ. Co. Mpls. MN 2000.

58

*This variety and diversity can involve natural and
social as well as spiritual differences. At the level
of nature, race, sex, and age are all differences
which must be included in the diversity of communion. No one should be excluded because of racial,
sexual or age differences.*

*...This is true about social differences as well: rich
and poor, powerful and weak, all should be accom-
modated in the community. The same must be said
about the variety of spiritual gifts. Not all in the
church are apostles, not all are teachers, not all
have the charisma of healing. Yet all of them are
needful of one another. Spiritual elitism—which
was condemned by St. Paul in Corinth—has never
ceased to tempt the churches. It is to be excluded
from an ecclesiology of communion.* *

NO SPIRITUAL ELITISM IN THE BODY

What Metropolitan John of Pergamon said about spiritual elitism has much to say about the fact that the
Orthodox Church is not just hierarchical but also conciliar.
Spiritual elitism is expressed in the false belief that only
patriarchs and bishops are needed for the governance and
administration of the body of Christ, the Church. The
clergy and the laypeople have no role except a passive
one. Yet, as St. Paul says in paraphrase, not all are patriarchs, not all are metropolitans, not all are bishops. There

* *The Church as Communion.* SVTGQ38. 1994. 3-16,8

are a multitude of other persons who also make up the body of Christ. That is why we believe that the Church is not just hierarchical. It is also conciliar, meaning that every baptized and chrismated person in the body has an active role to play in the governance and administration of the church. "The laity are the guardians of the faith," said our patriarchs in 1848. Spiritual elitism has no place in the body of Christ.

> *Now you are the body of Christ, and members individually. And God has appointed these in the church: first apostles, second prophets, third teachers, after that miracles, then gifts of healings, helps, administrations, varieties of tongues. Are all apostles? Are all prophets? Are all teachers? Are all workers of miracles? Do all have gifts of healings? Do all speak with tongues? Do all interpret?*
>
> *(1 Cor. 12:27-30)*

Spiritual elitism, the stomach saying to the rest of the body, "I don't need you", has no place in the body of Christ. The diversity of gifts is to be found in the entire body—clergy and laity.

In the words of Paul Evdokimov:

> *... the Church is always conciliar, "sobornal". Authority in the Church is never just from above, held by the clergy, but centered in Christ, enlivened by the Holy Spirit, in a community always including both pastors and people. The church's identity*

and truth are best expressed in the eucharistic assembly. *

The words of Fr. Thomas Hopko clarify the issue,

The Church is conciliar.... The laypeople are accountable to the clergy, and, in turn, the clergy are accountable to the laypeople. Because of the very nature of Christian life, there is no division between religious and secular, spiritual and material, clerical and lay. Everything is done in and for God, and by God's grace and power, by all of the members of the Body working together, each doing his or her part, according to his or her place, calling, and ministry within the one Body. **

THE PROTEST OF THE PARTS

Following is a perceptive poem entitled *The Protest of the Parts*:

I'm a foot and I am grand.
Who would want to be a hand?
I'm a hand with skill and grace;
I would never trade my place.
I'm an eye and I can see;
Every part should be like me.
No, ev'ry part should be like me;

---

* *L'Orthodoxie*, 123-66.
** *Speaking the Truth in Love*. Thomas Hopko. SVS Press. Crestwood, N.Y. 2004.

I'm a tough and useful knee.
I'm a mouth; a lovely voice
Of all the parts, I am the choice.
No, indeed, who wants to talk?
I'm a leg; I love to walk.
A leg can walk, but can it hear?
For that you have to be an ear!
But you can't smell with one of those.
To smell you have to have a nose.
Every part thinks it is best,
Looking down on all the rest.
Who will come and kill their pride?
Who will come and act as guide?

(S. Spencer)

"Now you are Christ's body, and each of you a limb or organ of it" (1 Cor. 12:27).

THE MOST VALUABLE PLAYER

Contrast this attitude with that of Joe Kapp, quarterback of the Minnesota Vikings, a team that played in the Super Bowl. At the end of the regular season the team voted him the Most Valuable Player. At a dinner where the award was given, Joe refused to accept it, saying, "Every member here is the most valuable player. No one could do anything without the rest of the players." He went back to his seat with the award still on the speaker's stand.

Isn't St. Paul telling us the same when he speaks of the

Church as the body of Christ?

In a team spirit, one is looking not so much for his own separate fulfillment, but for the good of the whole group or body. Those who have played basketball remember times when a certain player would desire to shoot the ball every time he got his hands on it. His desire was to build up his own score. While he may have achieved a higher score for himself, the team suffered overall.

IF ONE MEMBER SUFFERS, ALL SUFFER TOGETHER

A beautiful illustration of how all the members of the body work together to bring healing to a suffering member of the body occurred a few years ago at the Seattle Special Olympics.

Nine contestants, all physically or mentally disabled, assembled at the starting line for the 100-yard dash. At the gun they all started out, not exactly in a dash, but with the relish to run the race to the finish and win.

All, that is, except one boy who stumbled on the asphalt, tumbled over a couple of times, and began to cry. The other eight heard the boy cry. They slowed down and paused. Then they all turned around and went back. Every one of them. One girl with Down's Syndrome bent down, kissed him and said, "This will make it better." Then all nine linked arms and walked together to the finish line.

Everyone in the stadium stood, and the cheering went on for 10 minutes.

"If one member suffers, all suffer together; if one

member is honored, all rejoice together" (1 Cor. 12:26).

Though we may have differing gifts, though the labors of some may seem unnoticed while others seem to have been overly noticed, though some may appear to be doing all the work while others seem content to do no work at all, we are reminded by St. Paul, "But God has so adjusted the body, giving the greater honor to the inferior part, that there may be no discord in the body but that the members may have the same care for one another " (1 Cor. 12:24-25).

NOT ONE BUT MANY CARRY THE BALL

One day a football team was being badly beaten. The coach began to shout instructions from the sidelines. "Give the ball to Caldwell." Caldwell got the ball and was thrown for a five-yard loss. Again the coach yelled, "Give the ball to Caldwell." Caldwell tried the middle of the line and lost ten yards. Undaunted, the coach called again, "Give the ball to Caldwell." This time, Caldwell tried to pass but was sacked by the whole defensive line Then the quarterback called time out, came to the sidelines, and to the coach shouted, "Caldwell doesn't want the ball!" The effective life of the body of Christ requires that many "carry the ball". Not Caldwell all the time! It is never right to depend on one member of the team—be he patriarch, bishop, priest, deacon or layperson—to do all the work and all the thinking. Spiritual elitism has no place in the Body of Christ.

LINKED TOGETHER

When we are climbing a mountain, hardly anyone can climb to the top alone, by himself. But we can climb, go up *together* by linking ourselves with a rope. The ablest climber goes first and the rest make the climb after him, linked to him.

You cannot climb the mountain for me. I cannot climb it for you. We have to climb it ourselves. But, linked to one another with the ablest One, Jesus, leading, we can make the climb. Faith, prayer and the Eucharist are the ropes which link us to the Lead Climber, the Lord Jesus.

We are linked together in more ways than we realize. For example, it is not enough to pray, "Lord, protect me and mine." In order to protect me and mine, the Lord must also protect the others on the freeway. One accident up ahead, one careless move on the part of another driver, can involve me and mine in a serious accident. As members of the same body, we need to pray for one another because we are interdependent.

THE "ALLELON" PRINCIPLE OF THE NEW TESTAMENT

One of the most vivid ways the Lord Jesus reveals His intention for the church as a body is by a series of statements given about our responsibilities toward one another. The phrase "one another", as translated from the Greek word *allelon*, provides us with what someone calls the *allelon* principle of the New Testament. This principle provides us with a tremendous picture of what *koinonia* in the body looks like in action. Here is a list of those *allelon* statements from the New Testament, and what a list it is! In the body of Christ, we are to:

- wash one another's feet (John 13:14);
- love one another (John 13:34);
- be devoted to one another in brotherly love (Romans 12:10);
- give preference to one another in honor (Romans 12:10);
- be of the same mind toward one another (Romans 12:16; 15:5);
- stop judging one another (Romans 14:13);
- pursue the building up of one another (Romans 14:19);
- accept one another (Romans 15:7);
- admonish one another (Romans 15:14);
- greet one another (Romans 16:16);
- wait for one another (1 Corinthians 11:33);
- care for one another (1 Corinthians 12:25);
- serve one another through love (Galatians 5:13);
- bear one another's burdens (Galatians 6:2);
- show forebearance to one another (Ephesians 4:2);
- be kind to one another (Ephesians 4:32);
- forgive one another (Ephesians 4:32);
- speak to one another in psalms, hymns, and spiritual songs (Ephesians 5:19)
- be subject to one another (Ephesians 5:21);
- regard one another as more important (Philippians 2:3);
- do not lie to one another (Colossians 3:9);

- teach one another (Colossians 3:16);
- comfort one another (1 Thessalonians 4:18);
- encourage one another (1 Thessalonians 5:11);
- be at peace with one another (1 Thessalonians 5:13);
- pursue good to one another (1 Thessalonians 5:15);
- consider one another (Hebrews 10:25);
- do not speak against one another (James 4:11);
- do not complain against one another (James 5:9);
- confess your sins to one another (James 5:16);
- pray for one another (James 5:16);
- be hospitable to one another (Peter 4:9);
- clothe yourself with humility toward one another (1 Peter 5:5).

This is the way the members of the body love, support and care for one another. The word *allelon* in each of the above verses expresses the fact that as members of the one body of Christ, we belong to Him and to one another. Because we all constitute one body, we are to love, respect and care for one another, as we care for the members of our own body. "The eye cannot say to the hand, 'I have no need of you'" (1 Cor. 12:21).

We are to build up each other's faith. "If your brother is being caused sorrow by what you eat, you are no longer walking in love. Do not let what you eat cause the ruin of one for whom Christ died" (Rom. 14:15).

St. Clement of Rome in the first century (96 A.D.) expressed it this way:

Why is there strife, anger, dissension, schism, and war among you? Is not then the God we have one God, and is not Christ one, and is not the Spirit of grace infused in us one, and is not our vocation in Christ one? Why then do we tear and rend the members of Christ and rise against our own body and rush into such madness that we forget we are members of one another?

OUR OTHER FAMILY

It would make a great deal of difference if the idea that we are members of the same body of Christ would really get hold of us in the way we handle our possessions. It would show dynamically, for example, in the wills that Christians make, as well as in the lives they live. One woman called a pastor to her bedside before her death and told him she wished to discuss the problem of making out her will. The pastor asked, "To whom do you want to leave what you have?" She replied, "I shall leave it to my family." The pastor asked, "To which family do you refer?" She replied, "Why, what do you mean? I have only one family. I have a niece and a nephew." The pastor said to her, "Haven't you forgotten something? When you were baptized into Jesus Christ, God became your Father and Christ became your Elder Brother. Then every Christian in the world became your brother and your sister. You became a member of God's family, the body of Christ. Don't you think you should also mention in your will this other family of yours, the church? Somewhat taken aback, the woman said, "Why, I never thought of it that way." How many of us do?

One of the most embarrassing things a Christian can do is to leave a "pagan" will, with no acknowledgment that he/she belonged to God, to Christ, to the same body, the Church , and to others. As members of the body of Christ, we do indeed have more than one family.

WE FEEL EACH OTHER'S PAIN

"If one member suffers, all suffer together" (1 Cor. 12:26). Plato pointed out once that when our finger hurts we usually do not say, "My finger has a pain"; we say, "I have a pain." Within each one of us there is a personality that gives unity to all the many and varying parts of the body. So, every irritation, every bit of suffering, however small, is felt at the very center of our being. Fr. Alexander Elchaninov expressed the implications of this when he wrote, "And when one member suffers, all members suffer with it" (1 Cor. 12:26). This is said of the church. If we do not feel this shared pain, we are not within the church."*

The Church as the body of Christ is marked by the same kind of sensitivity. Hurt and suffering in any one of its members is felt by all of its members. Is not this the essence of *agape*, love?

St. Symeon the New Theologian felt this so keenly that he wrote, "I know a man who desired the salvation of his brethren so fervently that he often besought God with burning tears and with his whole heart .... that either his

* *Diary of a Russian Priest.* SVS Press. Crestwood, N.Y. 1967.

brethren might be saved with him, or that he might be condemned with them. For he was bound to them in the Holy Spirit by such a bond of love that he did not even wish to enter the Kingdom of Heaven, if to do so meant to be separated from them." How keenly he felt Paul's words, "If one member suffers, all suffer together."

It is for this reason that the Christian Church has always been in the very forefront of all ministries that help alleviate pain and suffering. The first asylum for the blind was founded by a Christian monk, Thalasius, and the first free dispensary by Apollonius, a Christian merchant. The first hospital of which there is any record was founded by a Christian woman, Fabiola.

During the great Decian persecution the church in Rome had under its care a great crowd of widows, orphans, blind, lame and sick folk. The heathen prefect broke into the church and demanded that the congregation hand over its treasures to the state. Laurentius the deacon pointed at the crowd of poor and sick and maimed and lonely and said: "These are the treasures of the church."

ALL FOR ONE

If you injure your hand, millions of white corpuscles rush through the blood stream to the open wound and lay down their lives fighting against the invading germs. If even the smallest toe hurts, the eye at once looks toward it, the fingers grasp it, the face frowns, the whole body bends to it, and all are concerned about this tiny member. When it is cared for, all the other members rejoice. All parts of the body rush to the aid of any single part of it, for the body is one. And, in the case of blindness, the other members of the body step in to compensate for the lack of sight.

What a beautiful picture of how God wants us to feel the pain of others and to care for even the least, the smallest and most insignificant member of the body of Christ, "the least of the brethren". "If one member suffers, we all suffer with it." If we do not share the pain of those small members of the body who are suffering— "the least of the brethren" —we are truly not within the body. It is a sign that we have separated ourselves from the body.

If a sensitive nerve is touched, it registers pain in the brain. Since our Lord is the Head of the Body, must He not feel every person's pain as His own? Perhaps this is why He said, "I was hungry and you fed me. I was sick and you visited me. I was in prison and you came to me."

FEELING THE BEGGAR'S PAIN

We are called upon to see Christ not only in every beggar but also to feel that beggar's pangs of hunger. St. Chrysostom wrote,

Do you want to honor Christ's body? Then do not scorn him in his nakedness, nor honor him here in the church with silken garments while neglecting him outside where he is cold and naked.... What good is it to weigh down Christ's table with golden cups (chalices) when he himself is dying of hunger? First, feed him when he is hungry; then use the means you have left to adorn his table ....

Apply this also to Christ when he comes along the road as a pilgrim, looking for shelter. You do not take him in as your guest, but you decorate floor and walls and the capitals of the pillars .... Once again, I am not forbidding you to supply these adornments; I am urging you to provide these other things as well, and indeed, to provide them first. Do not adorn the church and ignore your afflicted neighbors, for they are the most precious temples of all (Homily on Matthew 88:50).

"NOT DISCERNING THE BODY"

We read in 1 Cor. 11:29, "for everyone who eats and drinks without discerning the body eats and drinks judgment upon himself." Have we ever investigated to see what those words *without discerning the body* mean? To do this, we must go back to the Corinthian Church when those words were written by Paul. Preceding the Lord's Supper in those days a love-feast was served. Each disciple was supposed to put the food he had brought with him on a common table from which all shared alike. It was like a pot-luck dinner where each one brought food which all shared. But at Corinth, only the rich and their friends ate of their luxuries; while the poor in their midst went without food. They sat by hungry and watched the rich people eating. They did not share their food.

The eating and drinking unworthily arose from *not discerning the Body*. This does not refer only to the Lord's body which was broken for us; but also to His body, the Church. "The bread which we break, is it not a participation in the body of Christ? Because there is one bread, we who are many are one body" (1 Cor. 10:16,17). We eat and drink unworthily when we fail to discern, to realize that the poor, the weak, the hungry, the suffering who belong to Christ, belong also to us; that they are members with us of His body; that we are obligated to share our gifts with them. The one thing that renders us unworthy to approach the Cup is our refusal to *discern the body*, to not feel the hunger and pain of other members of the body and not to respond with love.

THE SACRAMENT OF THE NEIGHBOR

Olivier Clement, the noted French Orthodox theologian, singled out what he called one of the most ruinous schisms in the history of Christianity. He calls it "the schism between the sacrament of the altar and the sacrament of the brother." The same Christ Who comes to us in the sacrament of the altar (Eucharist) comes to us many times each day in the sacrament of the hurting, the hungry, the lonely, the imprisoned brother or sister. "I was hungry and you did not feed me …. Truly, I say to you as you did it not to one of the least of these my brethren, you did it not to me" (Matthew 25:34-40).

This great and sinful schism needs to be healed. The sacrament of the altar needs to be re-connected with the sacrament of the "least of the brethren". How can this happen? It happens when we leave church to go out to celebrate "the liturgy after the liturgy". We go out to continue the liturgy by ministering to the needs of the same Christ Who met us and Whom we received at the altar.

He is the same Christ Who appears before us as the hungry, the poor, the aged, the infirm, the starving, the stranger, the hurting and forgotten street person. This is the other body of Jesus that we need to "discern" as Paul writes to the Corinthians. In reality it is the same body as that which we encounter at the altar.

In many cases our first response is to turn away from "the least of these" because they remind us of our own frailty and mortality. Yet our role is clear:

> *The members of the body that seem to be weaker are indispensable, and those members of the body that we think less honorable we clothe with greater honor, and our less respectable members are treated with greater respect; whereas our more respectable members do not need this…. If one member suffers, all suffer together with it; if one member is honored, all rejoice with it (1 Cor. 12:22-24).*

Metropolitan Leonty, former head of the OCA Church in America, had a lovely way of breaking down the schism (separation) between the sacrament of the altar and the sacrament of the brother (sister). At the end of each service as worshippers came forward to kiss the cross he was holding, he would secretly slip some money to any person he knew who was indigent. He was ministering to the same Christ he encountered at the altar.

> *St. Anthony expresses this succinctly when he says that "our life and death lie with our brother and*

sister." A more recent saint, Silouan of Athos, puts it even more concisely: "Your brother is your life." We are saved together, by working out our salvation together as members of the body of Christ and as members of one another. How we relate with one another has everything to do with how we relate with God.*

How can we forget Alexis Khomiakov's classic statement on this theme:

When anyone of us falls, he falls alone, but no one is saved alone. He who is saved is saved in the Church, as a member of her, and in unity with all other members.

ABBA ZOSIMAS

Abba Zosimas wrote about how we are to minister to one another as members of the same body of Christ,

In effect, God has placed us in a body of many members, who have Christ our God as their head, as the Apostle said: "Just as the body is one and has many members, and the head of all is Christ" (1 Cor. 12:12). Therefore, when your brother afflicts you, he is hurting you like the hand or the eye of your body that suffers from some illness. Yet, even when we are in pain, we do not cut off

* *Soul Mending: The Art of Spiritual Direction.* John Chryssavgis. Holy Cross Orthodox Press. Brookline, MA. 2000

*our hand and throw it away; nor do we pull out
our eye; indeed, we consider the rejection of each
of these as being a very serious matter. Instead, we
mark these bodily members with the sign of Christ,
which is more precious than anything else, and
entreat the saints to pray for them, as well as offering our own fervent prayers to God on their behalf.
In addition to this, we apply medication and plas-
ter in order to heal the sore member. Therefore, in
the same way that you pray for your eye or your
hand in order to heal and no longer hurt, you
should also do for your brother (who like your
hand or eye is a member of your body).*

We are to treat the hurting and suffering members
of the body exactly as we treat our wounded hand or eye,
Zosimas says.

St. Paul's teaching about all of us being members of
the body of Christ must have inspired the famous saying,
"Never seek to know for whom the bell tolls; it tolls for
thee." That other person for whom the bell tolls is part of
me in the *koinonia* of the body. Thus, in the words of
John Donne, "No man is an island, entire of itself; every
man is a piece of the continent, a part of the main."

WE BELONG TO EACH OTHER

"So we, though many, are one body in Christ, and individually members one of another" (Romans 12:5). If we
are members "one of another", we belong to each other.
As members of the same body of Christ, we are all related

to each other in Christ and therefore responsible for each other in His Name.

Each one of us should be able to say to a fellow member of the body of Christ, "I need you. I need you to help me achieve my full potential in Christ. I need you to help me know myself. I need you to help me become more understanding, more patient, more faithful, more loving, more hopeful." We are responsible for each other since we are interdependent *in the koinonia of the body of Christ.*

St. Basil expressed this dramatically when he wrote: "The bread that remains uneaten in your house is the bread of the hungry. The tunic (coat) hanging in your wardrobe is the tunic of the naked. The footwear (shoe) that remains unused in your closet is that of the poor who go barefoot. The cash that you keep stashed away is money that belongs to the poor. You can tell how many injustices you commit by counting the benefits you could bestow."

Often in the past it was because we forgot that we belonged to each other as members of the same body that atheistic Communism was able to spread. Many years ago when peasants from the countryside came to a large city like Milan, in Italy, to find work, the church ignored them, did nothing for them, while the communists opened canteens for them, welcomed them and helped them find work. The church became an administrative institution and forgot the greatest commandment of its Master: love for the members of the body. "If one member suffers, all suffer together." If we do not feel their pain, it is because we are not true members of the body.

REMEMBER THE PEOPLE TO WHOM
WE BELONG

When we are tempted, the devil tries to get us to forget
that we belong to each other as members of the same
body. He suggests, for example, that the sin we are about
to commit is something that concerns us alone. This, of
course, is the big lie. We are not isolated islands. We are
all tied together in a body. We belong to each other. When
you and I fall, the whole church falls with us. So if nothing else restrains us when we are about to do something
wrong, let us remember our family, remember the people,
and the body and the Christ, to whom we belong. How
will it affect them? What will it do to them?

We belong to Christ and to each other. When someone
asks, "Can a person be a Christian outside the Church?"
we can ask that person, "Can a nose be a nose if it is
removed from the face?" It is only as we remain connected to the body that we can receive nourishment and
remain alive to be able to make our contribution for the
good of the whole body. In isolation we die; in interdependence (*koinonia*) we live.

The church as the body of Christ is an integral part of
God's plan of salvation. It is only in communion with
other believers in the body that each person comes to
know himself and is able to deepen one's communion with
God. We cannot make it alone, as solitary, lonely individuals. God counts on us to take one another by the hand
and move together through hard times. Christ works
through His body. It is through the community of faith,
through the body, through our sisters and brothers in

Christ, that God brings us through difficult times.

We belong to each other as members of the body of Christ. So "we, though many, are one body in Christ, and individually members one of another" (Romans 12:5).

CONNECTED WITH THE FOLKS BACK HOME

When U.S. troops were fighting in Korea, a journalist hitched a ride with a sergeant. As the jeep bounced along, the sergeant asked, "Are you just over from the states?" The journalist replied that he was. The soldier wanted to know what the people back home were thinking and saying about the war. At last the sergeant said, "You know, it's a funny thing about this business of morale. It's not what a lot of people think it is. It isn't beer, and it isn't USO shows with Bob Hope. Morale is the feeling that somehow you are connected up with the folks back home, and that they are connected up with you."

As members of the body of Christ we are indeed "connected up" with each other and with Christ. If this feeling of connectedness is a morale-builder to a soldier, how much more to us as Christians: to know that we are not isolated nobodies existing in a great vacuum of nothingness; but all of us together make up the one body of Christ and each one of us is a separate and necessary part of the body. "And the eye cannot say to the hand, 'I have no need of you'; nor again the head to the feet, 'I have no need of you'" (1 Cor. 12:21).

WHAT MAKES US A BODY?

We are made members of the body of Christ through the sacraments of Baptism, Chrismation and the Eucharist. Through Baptism we are attached to His Body as members. Through Chrismation the members of our body are sealed and anointed by the Holy Spirit, dedicated to the service of God. Through Holy Communion Jesus comes to live in His members to nourish them with His divine power and presence. "He who eats my flesh and drinks my blood lives in Me and I in him" (John 6:56). In the Eucharist we become what we receive. The Eucharist *re-members* us to Christ and to one another. In the words of Afanasiev, "The Eucharist makes the Church."

The community of God's people who eat the same bread, i.e., the same body of Christ, become the body of Christ. "The bread which we break, is it not a communion of the body of Christ? For as there is one single bread, so we become one single body" (1 Cor. 10:17). In the words of St. John of Damascus, "Since we partake of one bread, we all become one body of Christ and one blood, and members one of another, being of one body with Christ."

THE EUCHARIST IS BASIC TO THE FORMATION OF THE BODY

Fr. Nicolas Afanasiev, noted scholar of Eucharistic ecclesiology, considers the Eucharist basic to the formation of the body of Christ:

The church was established by Christ at the Last Supper and came into existence on the day of Pentecost, when the first Eucharist was celebrated by the disciples…. On the day of Pentecost, the disciples were filled with the Spirit…. The disciples become "one body" in the Eucharist, which is accomplished in the Spirit and through the Spirit…. The Eucharist is the center towards which everything aims and in which everything meets. The Body of Christ is realized only in the Eucharist. *

In the words of Fr. Patrick Reardon:

The final and defining purpose of the epicletic summoning of the Holy Spirit, then is not the consecration of bread and wine, but the consecration of human beings. The risen Christ does not assume the form of the consecrated bread and wine in order to hide in a tabernacle, but in order to be eaten and drunk, that He may abide in us and we in Him (John 6:56). **

The purpose of the Holy Spirit in the liturgy is to consecrate not just the bread and the wine, but all of the communicants, transfiguring us, rendering us true members of the body of Christ. Thus, the fact that the very blood of

---

* *The Lord's Supper,* hereafter LS (Trapeza Gospodnia [Paris: YMCA Press, 1952], in Russian), trans. Michael J. Lewis (Crestwood, NY: St. Vladimir's Orthodox Theological Seminary, 1988), 1-2.
** *Again Magazine.* Vol. 24, No. 3

Jesus flows in our veins through the Eucharist, makes every member of our body a member of Christ's body. Truly, He has no hands or feet but ours to accomplish His work in the world today.

Thus, we are called to be real, live members of a living body, the head of which is the Lord Jesus—a body that St. Ignatius of Antioch (first century) called "the total Christ, head and body together".

The other sacrament that makes us members of the body of Christ is baptism through which we are grafted into the body of Christ, becoming members of His body. Each baptized Christian thus becomes an extension of Christ. We become other Christs in the world. We become His eyes, His hands, His tongue, His feet. Christ has chosen to work in the world through us—the members of His body. It is our special responsibility as baptized Christians to let Christ be present wherever we ourselves are stationed in the world as baptized Christians.

The Eucharist is also called *Koinonia* [communion] and rightly so, for by it we have communion with Christ— and by it we also have communion and are made one with each other, because we are part of the one body.

INGESTING AND DIGESTING
THE WORD OF GOD

When Israel's great prophets were called, God initiated them through a powerful ritual. They were asked to physically eat the scroll of the law, i.e., their scriptures. The idea was that they should digest the word of God and turn it into their own flesh so that people would be able to see the word of God in a living body rather than on a dead parchment. So it is that through the Eucharist and the written word of God, we ingest and digest Jesus so that He becomes flesh in our bodies. Thus people will not have to read the Bible to see what God is like. They would need only to see Him in us. We are "light, salt and yeast", said Jesus.

Since we have used St. Paul's example of the body as an example of the *koinonia* or communion we experience as members of Christ and of one another, I share with you the following words by J. Robinson, a British theologian, since they summarize the fullness of scriptural meaning inherent in the powerful scriptural word, body:

It is from the body of sin and death that we are delivered; it is through the body of Christ on the Cross that we are saved; it is into His body the Church that we are incorporated; it is by His body in the Eucharist that this community (body) is sustained; it is in our body that its new life has to be manifested; it is to a resurrection of this body to the likeness of His glorious body that we are destined.

TOUCHING AND TASTING THE NEW LIFE

It is not just the soul that is saved and glorified. It is the soul together with the body. Christianity is a very materialistic faith.

The message of Pascha, for example, is announced to us in the body, the Church. What happens to us in the

Church happens to us through our bodies. We are washed of our sins bodily through the waters of baptism. We are buried bodily in the waters of baptism and raised with Christ to newness of life. But our problem is that we do not always live as people washed in the resurrection life. Our journey from baptism through life is marked with sin and despair. We need nourishment and strength for the journey. We need forgiveness. And that is why we keep bringing our bodies to Christ's table. "This is my body given for you," we hear Jesus promise. "This is my blood shed for you." We eat and we drink. In and through the Eucharist our bodies are bathed and nourished with resurrection life. We touch and taste new life. The hope of Pascha flows into our bodies and we leave the table revived. Our bodies have fed upon the resurrection. Our connection with the body of Christ is revived and restored.

WE BECOME CHRIST'S LIMBS

St. Symeon the New Theologian describes what happens to our body when we feed on Christ through the Eucharist and His word:

We become Christ's limbs or members, and Christ becomes our members…. Unworthy though I be, my hand and foot are Christ. I move my hand, and my hand is wholly Christ, for God's divinity is united inseparably to me. I move my foot, and lo! It glows like God Himself….

As members of His body, united with Christ, we become "partakers of divine nature". As Jesus, a member our body, is now seated at the right hand of God's throne, so we as members of the same Body shall be seated there with Him. For, in a living organism is it ever possible for the head to be separated from the body? Has not Christ—the Head—already ascended with His human nature (body) to the right hand of the Father where He awaits us? That is where we belong! That is our destiny!

LESSONS FROM THE FLYING GEESE

We find a beautiful sense of *koinonia*, communion, interdependence in the animal kingdom among the geese. It mirrors what should be happening among the members of the body of Christ.

Next time you see geese heading south for the winter, flying along in V formation, you might be interested in knowing what science has discovered about why they fly that way. As each bird flaps its wings, it creates an uplift for the bird immediately following. By flying in V forma-tion, the whole flock adds at least 71% greater flying range than if each bird flew on its own. And so it is that Christians who share a common direction and a sense of *koinonia*, community, can get where they are going quick-er and easier because they are traveling on the thrust and uplift of one another.

Whenever a bird falls out of formation, it suddenly feels the drag and resistance of trying to go it alone, and quickly gets back into formation, to take advantage of the lifting power of the bird immediately in front. If we

Christians have as much sense as the geese, we will stay in formation with those who are headed in the same direction. When the lead bird gets tired, it rotates to the back and another bird flies point. And so with us. It pays to take turns doing hard jobs with people at church as with geese. They rotate. And let's remember that the geese are constantly honking from behind to encourage those up front to keep up their speed. They encourage those ahead for the good job they're doing.

Finally, when a goose gets sick, or is wounded by gunshot and falls out, two geese fall out of formation and follow him down to help and protect him. They stay with him until he is able to fly, or until he is dead; and then they launch out on their own or with another formation to eventually catch up with their original group.

They are acting as members of a body. What an example for us as members of Christ's body whom Christ loves so dearly that He said, "Father, I desire that they also, whom thou hast given me, may be with me where I am, to behold my glory which thou hast given me in thy love for me before the foundation of the world" (John 17:24).

PRAYER

Christ – here is my brain – think through it.
Christ – here is my face – glow through it.
Christ – here are my eyes – look at people through them.
Christ – here is my heart – love people with it.

PART TWO

Laity and Hierarchy: Their Respective Roles As Members of the Body of Christ

The Church is not the bishop alone, or the priest alone, or the laity alone. It is the bishop, priests and laity working together in synergy, as one body. For, "we are laborers together with God" (1 Cor. 3:8).

MEMBERS OF CHRIST'S BODY: LAITY AND HIERARCHY

The church is not the bishop alone, or the priest alone, or the laity alone. The church is bishop, priest, and lay people working together in synergy. For, "we are laborers together with God" (1 Cor. 3:9). Clergy and laity together constitute the body of Christ, the Church.

St. Peter was speaking to all Christians, clergy and laity alike, when he wrote, "You are a chosen race and a royal priesthood." For, all who were "baptized into Christ have put on Christ," writes St. Paul. Following baptism we are anointed with Holy Chrism, i.e., we are ordained into the "royal priesthood of believers" to work along with the bishops and priests as one body in the many ministries of the Church.

Fr. Alexander Schmemann explains,

Chrismation gives us the positive power and grace to be Christians, to act as Christians, to build together the Church of God and be responsible participants in the life of the Church. In this sacrament we pray that the newly baptized be: "an honorable member of God's Church, a consecrated vessel, a child of light, an heir of God's kingdom", that "having preserved the gift of the Holy Spirit and increased the measure of grace committed unto him, he may receive the prize of his high calling and be numbered with the first born whose names are written in heaven".

He goes on to say that the lay people actually co-celebrate the liturgy with the priest:

The layman is in a very direct way the co-celebrant of the priest, the latter offering to God the prayers of the Church, representing all people, speaking on their behalf. One illustration of this co-celebration may be helpful; the word Amen, to which we are so used, that we really pay no attention to it. And yet it is a crucial word. No prayer, no sacrifice, no blessing is ever given in the Church without being sanctioned by the Amen which means an approval, agreement, participation. To say Amen to anything means that I make it mine, that I give my consent to it.... And "Amen" is indeed the Word of the laity in the Church, expressing the function of the laity as the People of God, which freely and joyfully accepts the Divine offer, sanctions it with its consent. There is really no service, no liturgy without the Amen of those who have been ordained to serve God as community, as Church. *

Metropolitan John (Zizioulas) of Pergamon observes,

The bishop is ordained for a particular Church to be its head and the center of its unity. In the exercise of his ministry he is the "one" who nevertheless cannot be conceived of without the "many", his community. The bishop is the head, but as such

---

* *Clergy and Laity in the Orthodox Church.* Alexander Schmemann. Published by Schmemann. Org.

he is conditioned by the "body"; he cannot exercise his authority except in communion with his faithful. Just as he cannot celebrate the Eucharist without the synaxis of his people, his whole ministry requires the consensus fidelium, the "Amen" of the community. The converse is equally true; there is no community without a head, the bishop, and nothing can be done without him. *

HIERARCHICAL AND CONCILIAR

This demonstrates that the Orthodox Church is not only hierarchical but also conciliar. It meets together as the body of Christ and decides on matters of faith and life in councils under the guidance of the Holy Spirit. It is to be noted that decisions of such councils can be, and have been, rejected in the past by the consensus of the Church, which includes the laity.

Professor Lewis J. Patsavos, Professor of Canon Law, explains what "conciliar" means:

"Hierarchical" means made up of bishops. Consequently, ours is a Church made up of bishops in communion with each other, who share authority and dialogue when they meet in council. Our Church is also a conciliar Church in which her bishops exercise authority in the name of their council (synod). Conciliarity, however, is not confined to bishops alone. It is expressed in every act

---

* *Sourozh*, Spring 2001.

of communion between an archbishop and bishops,
between bishop and presbyters (priests), between a
priest and his parishioners, and among parish-
ioners themselves. Dialogue reflects this under-
standing of the Church as conciliar.

As conciliar, the Church is synodal, i.e., hierarchs of the Church meet in synods to decide on church matters. Yet their power is not absolute. Each bishop casts one vote in a process that is quite democratic.

In 1990, the Holy Cross Orthodox Press published the *Report to His Eminence Archbishop Iakovos* by the Commission to Establish the Theological Agenda for the future of the Greek Orthodox Archdiocese. The report made the following statement about the conciliar aspect of the Church, "Our concern with authority and leadership is based on the theological premise that the Church is truly, and at its best, a conciliar reality."

Fr. Theodore Stylianopoulos writes that the Orthodox Church is a:

...Church which rejects both clericalism and con-
gregationalism. It is shepherded by a hierarchy
defined by conciliarity and the synodical system.
The Church lives by a synergy of gifts and talents
of clergy and laity, together making up God's peo-
ple, all mutually supportive and accountable, all
serving as the conscience of the Church, all being
the guardians of the faith....

The principle of conciliarity is of such depth and significance in Orthodoxy that a number of Orthodox theologians have connected it with the life of God as Holy Trinity. Just as in the life of God, Father, Son and Holy Spirit, there is mutual indwelling, shared communion, and plenitude of love, so also in the life of the Church there should be free self-giving, full sharing and mutual service reflecting the presence and light of the Holy Trinity. *

This is what must have prompted Metropolitan Anthony Bloom to say once that conciliarity is "the heart-beat of life in the Holy Spirit." **

The Holy Spirit established not only the episcopate and the presbyters, but even more basically the royal priesthood of the faithful. Together they constitute the Church—not just the bishops, not just the priests, not just the laity—but the *Koinonia* of the entire body of Christ guided and indwelt by the Holy Spirit.

In the Church writes Fr. Schmemann, "There is neither blind obedience nor democracy, but a free and joyful acceptance of what is true, noble, constructive and con-ducive of the Divine love and salvation."

* *The Way of Christ.* Theodore Stylianopoulos. Holy Cross Orthodox Press. Brookline, MA. 2002.
** *Sourozh Magazine.*

WHAT HAPPENS WHEN A BISHOP ERRS?

Dr. Charles T. Lelon in a superb lecture a few years ago asked the question:

But when a bishop is mistaken, where do we turn to discern the True Faith? Simply to other bishops. It is still the episcopacy that teaches the Faith, but our ecclesiology of communion does not permit a single bishop to define the Faith. He must consult with nearby bishops. Canon 4 of Nicea specifies that the consecration of bishops requires at least three other bishops, but preferably all the bishops in the province. Even during the consecration of a bishop, the Holy Spirit does not pass from one bishop to the other; the Spirit passes through many to the one. "For wherever two or three have gathered in my name, I am there among them" (Mt. 18:20). The synodical or conciliar nature of the Orthodox Church is one of its most striking features. There is no single bishop, as in the Roman Catholic tradition, that exercises authority over the entire Church. All bishops are equals in their teaching ministry. Acts 15 is remarkable evidence of the Apostolic foundation for the conciliar approach to defining dogma in the face of crisis. For two thousand years the Orthodox Church has relied on councils to define and proclaim the Faith.

THE CHURCH AS COMMUNION

It is true that the Church is not a democracy. It is not democratic precisely because it supersedes democracy. As the body of Christ, the Church is a communion of all its members, held together not by one patriarch or pope, but by the double bond of unity in faith and communion in the sacraments, especially the Eucharist. It is a communion energized and animated by the Holy Trinity.

The question is asked, "Can local synods of bishops be relied upon as guarantors of the true faith?" The answer comes from history itself, which tells us that local councils have erred in the past, i.e., the second council of Ephesus in 449 was rejected by the Church.

Even great Councils convened as "Ecumenical" were found to be in error and rejected. The seven councils now accepted as Ecumenical are considered as such because they were received and validated universally by the entire body of Christ, the Church at large. In some instances, Sacred Tradition confirmed and upheld the views of the minority, even a minority of one, as in the case of St. Maximos the Confessor. He was condemned as a heretic for upholding a teaching that the Church later acknowledged as Orthodox. Following his death, he was canonized a saint.

THE CONSCIENCE OF THE CHURCH

Dr. Lewis J. Patsavos describes the role that the lay people played in the Ecumenical Councils:

From the Apostolic Synod of the first century in Jerusalem to the ecumenical synods and beyond, representatives of the laity were always present as a living witness to the Church's conscience of which they are an integral part. Their role was passive; about this there can be no doubt. They were there, often upon the invitation of the episcopacy, to make known the mind of the people—but they were there. And when the bishops, who alone have the right, cast their vote, it was more often than not with the approbation of the laity.*

The bishop must never be isolated from his flock if he is to know the mind of the Church, and neither should the flock be separated from its shepherd.

They are called to work together as members of the one body of Christ.

The work of governing Christ's Church is not to be done behind closed doors by the hierarchy alone and then imposed upon the other members of the body without considering the laity. This is tantamount to the eye saying to the other members of the body, "I have no need of you" (1 Cor. 12:21).

In the words of Fr. Thomas Hopko,

The Church is neither a democracy nor a hierocracy. Its members, clergy and laypeople, have no powers or rights. They have only gifts and services. They conquer only by truth and love in sacrifi-

* *The Role of the Priest and the Apostolate of the Laity.* Edited by N. M. Vaporis. 1982. HCO Press, Brookline MA.

cial suffering with their crucified Christ, their sole Savior and Judge.[*]

LAITY: GUARDIANS OF THE FAITH

As members of the body of Christ, the laity have an important role to play in the Church. They are part of the communion of the body of Christ working in synergy with the hierarchy in the mission and governance of the Church. As the Orthodox Patriarchs wrote in an 1848 letter sent to Pope Pius 9th:

> *Among us, neither Patriarch nor Councils, could ever introduce new teaching, for the guardian of religion is the very body of the Church, that is, the people itself.*

Each lay person is ordained to be a guardian, protector and propagator of the Faith. In the words of the late Fr. John Meyendorff:

> *A conciliar decree by the bishops needed the reception of the entire Church to be considered a true expression of tradition…. All this indicates that authority in the Church neither suppresses nor diminishes freedom…. The Christian notion of authority excludes blind obedience and presupposes free and responsible participation of all in the common life of the Body.*

[*] *Speaking the Truth in Love.* Thomas Hopko. SVS Press. Crestwood, N.Y. 2004.

Dr. Valerie Karras, noted Orthodox academician, has emphasized that history contains many examples of the laity's "stubborn refusal" to accept without discussion whatever the hierarchy decreed. She has pointed out that at certain crucial periods in history "lay activism saved Orthodoxy from heresy itself." This happened when the laity played a major role in restoring the veneration of icons, and in refusing to accept Papal supremacy when most hierarchs desired to do so.

As Dr. Lewis J. Patsavos writes, "We can only know that a particular gathering is genuinely ecumenical and infallible if it has been subsequently accepted as such by the whole Church."

NO DIVISION BETWEEN TEACHING CHURCH AND TAUGHT CHURCH

In Orthodoxy there is no division between a "Teaching Church" and a "Taught Church", i.e., the hierarchy teaches (actively) while the laity sit back and are taught (passively). The formula of the Apostolic Council, "It has seemed good to the Holy Spirit and to us" (Acts 15:28), is the formula of every Ecumenical Council and establishes the basis of the conciliar structure of the Orthodox understanding of the Church.

Metropolitan Filaret defined this as the *sobornost* principle, i.e., "All together and all in succession are incorporated by God into one Church, which is the true repository of sacred tradition. The 'people' signifies the hierarchy and the faithful together, constituting inseparable, complementary elements of the Body. This does away with any division into 'Teaching Church', still more into 'Taught Church'…. The whole Church is *teaching* and *taught* at the same time."

Paul Evdokimov adds "…there exists no separation between the teaching Church and the Church taught. It is the whole Church that teaches the Church, just as it is in the whole of its teaching that the Gospel is addressed to each and every one."

LAY PEOPLE AS APOSTOLIC BEINGS

It is not by accident that the last verses of St. Matthew's Gospel are read at the baptismal service: "Go therefore and make disciples of all nations." It is by this reading that the great commission is addressed to every baptized and chrismated person who now becomes "an apostolic being at baptism," as Paul Evdokimov notes, called to give constant testimony to Christ through his life and works.

Archbishop Anthony Bloom expressed the high status of the laity in the Orthodox Church as the "royal priesthood" when he said once, upon being asked who he was: "I am a layman who happens to be an archbishop."

LAY PEOPLE ARE ORDAINED

The Orthodox Church considers lay people together with bishops and priests as God's people. They are all ordained into the "royal priesthood of believers" through the Sacrament of Chrismation. Fr. Alexander Schmemann emphasized this when he wrote,

We are accustomed to think of "ordination" as precisely the distinctive mark of clergy. There are the ordained and the laity, the non-ordained Christians.   Here again, however, Orthodoxy differs from Western "clericalism," be it Roman Catholic or Protestant. If ordination means primarily the bestowing of the gifts of the Holy Spirit for the fulfillment of our vocation as Christians and members of the Church, each layman becomes a layman—laikos—through ordination. We find it in the Sacrament of Holy Chrism, which follows Baptism. Why are there two, and not just one, sacraments of entrance into the Church? Because if Baptism restores in us our true human nature, obscured by sin, Chrismation gives us the positive power and grace to be Christians, to act as Christians, to build together the Church of God and be responsible participants in the life of the Church."

All Christians are called through their baptismal priesthood to do the work of the Church and to be the Church. They are called not just to go to Church, but to be the Church wherever they go.

HOLY CHRISM: THE SACRAMENT OF UNIVER-SAL PRIESTHOOD

Paul Evdokimov makes it plain that "every baptized person is sealed with the gifts, anointed with the Holy Spirit in his very essence. Every lay person is the priest of his or her existence, offering in sacrifice (to God) his entire life and existence."

Evdokimov elaborates on the importance of the Sacrament of Chrismation calling it "the sacrament of universal priesthood.... The anointing (Chrismation) is a sacrament of strength which arms us as soldiers and athletes for Christ.... The sign of the cross made with chrism on all parts of the body symbolizes the tongues of fire of Pentecost.... Each baptized person is an entirely charismatic being.... The rite of tonsure is identical with that performed for one entering monastic life.... Its symbolic meaning is unmistakable—it is the total offering of one's life."*

To say, then, that the position of lay people in the Church is passive, Evdokimov states, is "a flagrant contradiction of what the Church Fathers teach."

CALLED TO AN ACTIVE NOT PASSIVE ROLE

Thus, according to St. Paul, the Church is not a bus that is being driven by the priest in which the lay members are the passengers and where their role is to sit quietly and be taken to their destination in heaven.

* *Ages o f the Spiritual Life*. Paul Evdokimov. SVS Press. Crestwood, N.Y. 1998.

The best refutation of this concept of the Church is St. Paul with his view of the Church as a body where each member, however insignificant, has a vital function to perform. Marshall McLuhan's words ring true here, "There are no passengers on spaceship earth. We are all crew."

If the Church is to function efficiently as a body, the priest is not a bus driver but more like a coach whose purpose is to train the members of the team—the laity—to offer service to God. He seeks to discover, develop, encourage, and cultivate the talents that lie dormant in his flock. He seeks to utilize them in Christian witness and ministry to the needy and suffering for the building up of the Body of Christ.

The charisma we need to look for today in ordained clergy is the gift of discernment, i.e., the ability to recognize the Holy Spirit's *charismata* (gifts) in every person in the congregation and see that such *charismata* are developed and used for God's glory and His work through the Church.

EXAMPLES OF LAY PARTICIPATION

Following are some examples of how the laity have participated in the mission of the Church.

We will begin with some rather recent examples.

Prior to 1923, the Ecumenical Patriarch was elected by a mixed council of eight lay people and four metropolitans.

Patriarch Alexius II of Moscow was elected by 66 bishops, 66 priests and 66 lay people, representing the 66 dioceses of Russia.

Archbishop Chrysostom of Cyprus and Patriarch Peter VII of Alexandria were elected with lay participation.

In early Christian history, the people elected their bishops. For example, we read in the early Christian document called the *Didache*: "You must, then, elect for yourselves bishops and deacons who are a credit to the Lord, men who are gentle, generous, faithful, and well-tried."

Even St. Cyprian, a strong defender of the episcopate, said, in speaking to his clergy, "From the beginning of my episcopate I decided to do nothing…without your advice and the consent of the people."

When St. Augustine wanted to name his successor, he presented his nominee to the congregation and asked, "I need your assent to this; show me some agreement by your acclaim." The people proclaimed, "So be it."

There is even a fifth century example of a bishop, Rusticus, Bishop of Narbonne, who ordained his archdeacon and sent him to the people of Beziers as their new bishop. But Rusticus had neglected to consult with the people of Beziers, who promptly sent the new bishop back to Rusticus.

The Apostolic Constitution writes concerning the role of the laity in the selection of a bishop:

> *Let the bishop be ordained after he has been chosen by the people. When someone pleasing to all has been named, let the people assemble on the Lord's Day with all the presbyters and with such bishops as may be present. All giving assent, the bishops shall lay hands on him, and the presbytery shall stand by in silence. Indeed, all shall remain*

silent, praying in their hearts for the descent of the Spirit.

There is a venerable precedent for a role by the laity in the selection of bishops. Such involvement can help ensure that future bishops are pastors, prophets, men of honor and integrity and not mere management functionaries.

In the words of Fr. John Chrysavvgis:

Ecclesiastical authority must be seen in terms of service and not rule; in relation to "diakonia" and dialogue, not domination. In order, however, for this to occur, the faithful must be regarded as gifted people of God, and not manipulated as objects or "sheep" to be taken for granted.

THE ROLE OF THE LAITY IN THE LITURGY

The active role of the laity is most evident in the liturgy, a Greek word (*leitourgia*) which means a common action in which the responsible participation of everyone is essential. Fr. Alexander Schmemann highlighted the active participation of the laity in the liturgy when he wrote:

*All prayers in the Orthodox Church are always written in terms of the plural **we**. We offer, we pray, we thank, we adore, we enter, we ascend, we receive. The layman is in a very direct way the co-celebrant of the priest, the latter offering to God* *the prayers of the Church,* **representing** *all people, speaking on their behalf.*

THE ACTIVE ROLE OF THE LAITY IN THE PROCESS OF CANONIZATION

The laity also play an active role in the selection of saints in the Orthodox Church. It is not the decision of some committee of bishops that declares one a saint, after which the believers merely accept the saint, passively, because of the committee's decision. It is the other way around, from the bottom up rather than from the top down. Thus, it is the lay people who initiate the process of sainthood in the Orthodox Church. The lay people submit the name of a potential saint to the bishops who then investigate and prayerfully deliberate whether or not to declare that person a saint.

Of course, the laity's participation in the mission of the Church is limited to specific areas. For example, they may not define the faith. That responsibility belongs to the bishops of the Church collectively in an Ecumenical Council. Yet even the bishops' decision must ultimately be accepted by the entire Body of Christ which includes the laity. It is the responsibility of the laity to guard, protect, and propagate the Faith.

THE LAITY'S ROLE DIMINISHED

It must be noted that the role of the laity in the Church was diminished when the Ottoman Empire set out to use the bishops of the Church as an instrument of control over the subject Orthodox population. The role of the laity was weakened as the bishops were given temporal and political power. But such is not the true tradition of Orthodoxy which has always, through the sacraments of initiation, bestowed upon the laity an important position with many privileges and responsibilities. Unfortunately many hierarchs during this period of Ottoman occupation began acting like despots instead of good shepherds.

Fr. Thomas Hopko explains that "during the five hundred years of Turkish rule, the (Orthodox) bishops were given civil powers over the Christian laity. They collected taxes, controlled behavior, judged disputes, and generally were answerable for the actions of their people to the Turkish rulers…. They also adopted all the insignia of the Christian lay rulers of the former empire. They wore the Turkish judicial robe *(riasson)*. They carried staffs and stood on eagle rugs and sat on the thrones formerly used by imperial civil authorities. They grew long hair, which was a sign of secular power in the Christian empire in which the clergy's hair was tonsured. They wore imperial crowns in church, and the imperial vestment *(sakkos)*. In a word, the bishops, and by extension the clergy, became rulers over the total life of the Christian laity."[*]

GOOD SHEPHERDS NOT ETHNARCHS

A contemporary example of such abuse of the office of bishop traceable to the period of Ottoman rule, when the Moslem rulers designated bishops to be ethnarchs, is

[*] *Speaking the Truth in Love*. Thomas Hopko. SVS Press. Crestwood, N.Y. 2004.

that of the late Archbishop Makarios of Cyprus. A Cypriot professor, the noted author Dr. Kyriacos C. Markides, documents this in his excellent book, *The Mountain of Silence*:

I lamented that Cyprus would have been different and perhaps more peaceful had the spirit of Athonite spirituality dominated the Cyprus church, particularly during those turbulent years of the 1950's. But, alas, there was none of that among the higher clergy. On the contrary, the then Archbishop Makarios ("the Blessed One"), ignoring Heaven completely, turned out to be more of a nationalist warrior than a man of God. For historical reasons that go back to the four centuries of Ottoman rule which preceded the British, the then archbishop was also the Ethnarch, the religious and national leader of the Greek Cypriots, an anachronistic and in retrospect destructive role reminiscent of the warrior popes of medieval Europe. As Ethnarch he led the Enosis movement with vigor but without any trace of the Ghandhian spirit of nonviolent resistance. Worst of all, ignoring the essence of the Christian message, it was he who conspired to clandestinely bring to the island a Cypriot-born Greek colonel with a well-known violent past to set up E.O.K.A. and wage a guerrilla campaign against the British colonial government. It was a grim, corrupting legacy that opened a Pandora's box, poisoning the lives of generations of Cypriots.*

* *The Mountain of Silence.* Kyriacos C. Markides. Doubleday Co., N.Y., 2001.

By accepting the Ottoman offer of having bishops serve as ethnarchs following the fall of Byzantium, the Church assumed attributes which belonged to the Byzantine emperor—not to Christ.

BARNACLES IN THE CHURCH

An ancient symbol used for the Church is that of a ship, the ship of salvation that leads to heaven and union with Christ. As barnacles accumulate on ships, however, the same happens with the Church.

We know that barnacles on a ship slow it down considerably and cost millions of dollars in extra fuel consumption. As a result, ships have to be dry-docked regularly to have their hulls sandblasted with powerful jackhammers.

Over the centuries similar barnacles have accumulated on the hull of the ship called the Church. They need to be sandblasted away because they impede the Church's mission. One such barnacle is the one imposed upon the office of bishop by the Ottoman Turks. We need to discard the notion of the hierarchy as despots wearing kingly crowns and the emperor's regal vestments, and restore the bishop to what Christ calls him to be: a footwasher and good shepherd who gives his life for the flock: "…the sheep hear his voice, and he calls his own sheep by name and leads them out…and the sheep follow him for they know his voice. A stranger they will not follow, but they will flee from him, for they do not know the voice of strangers" (John 10:3-5).

EACH MEMBER: A VOTIVE LIGHT

As good shepherds, bishops are called to work in concert with the other members of the body of Christ, the presbyters, deacons and laypeople. I share with you a beautiful story that illustrates the role of the members of the body of Christ.

In a village church in Tavancore, India, there is a wonderful brass lamp. It has about 100 slender arms hanging down from the ceiling. At the end of each is a cup that is filled with oil, and also contains a wick. Each family of the congregation brings its house lamp, and accordingly the church is lighted to the degree of the faithfulness of its worshipers. At the close of evening worship services, people come up to take their lamp to help guide them home through the night. It is a beautiful sight to watch the worshipers depart, and to see the many lights go out in different directions, pushing aside the darkness as they press on.

The darkness of the world would vanish if the members of the body of Christ would, as they leave church, go out into every area of life and let the light of their faith shine brightly and unashamedly. As we worship in church, commune at the Lord's table, pray, and hear the Word of God, we bring ourselves to where the Lord Jesus kindles and lights the votive light in our souls that we may live and walk as children of light in this sin-darkened world.

When asked why his church was so vibrantly active for the Lord, one priest said, "We worship and preach Christ on Sunday; we light our candles, and we have 450 members who take the lit candles and carry them out with

them on Monday, letting them shine wherever they go."
"Let your light so shine before people that they may see
your good works and glorify your Father in heaven," said
Jesus.

SERVANT LEADERSHIP

In Byzantium the emperor was regarded as "equal to
the apostles, God's Vice-Regent on earth." He held the
life of every one of his subjects in the hollow of his hand.

When the bishops took over the emperor's crown,
vestments and other exotic regalia after the fall of
Byzantium, some of them also assumed the emperor's
autocratic manner. The laity became "subjects in the hollow of their hands" instead of God's flock to be nurtured
and fed as Jesus commanded, "Feed my sheep."

This is a far cry from the servant leadership practiced
by Jesus who set the example for all of us, hierarchs, presbyters, deacons, monks, and laity—by washing the feet of
His disciples—a task reserved at that time for the lowest
slave on the totem pole. In fact, the New Testament Greek
word for bishop—*episcopos*—referred to the one who was
the chief of slaves in a household. It was the duty of the
episcopos to oversee the slaves below him. He owned
nothing. He merely managed his master's property.

Thus, the followers of Jesus, beginning with our leaders, the hierarchs, are called to be servants not monarchs.
"If anyone wants to be first, let him be a servant of all,"
said Jesus. The true calling of the hierarchy is to be found
in humble service, servant leadership. In fact, the higher
the servant is in rank and titles, the lower should be the

service he performs. He should be the one who performs the humblest service just as our True Leader, the Lord Jesus, emptied Himself for us, becoming not just a servant but a slave so that by His emptiness, His poverty, we might become rich.

Thus when we speak of hierarchy in the church, we need to focus on the original and true Hierarch—Jesus. His was a hierarchy of service, a hierarchy of humility, a hierarchy of washing feet, a hierarchy of love, a hierarchy of sacrifice, a hierarchy in which there was no domination, no power. God chose to be powerless, even to the point of giving us the right to say "no" to Him. But God in Christ had another fine quality of leadership—not power which is the ability to coerce, but authority, which is the ability to convince. And therein lies a very great difference. "No man ever spoke as this man," it was said of Jesus. "To whom shall we go, Lord," said the disciples, "You alone have words of eternal life." "He spoke as one who had authority"—the authority of God.

All of what we have written can be achieved only if we remember what St. Paul said in First Corinthians about the Church being the body of Christ. He drew a picture of the unity that exists in the body where each member knows its place and performs its duty without envy or strife. When the tiniest limb or organ ceases to function, the whole body suffers. It is so with the Church. When all members work together in love, the Church becomes vibrant, living, and God is glorified.

*But Jesus called them to Himself and said to them,
"You know that those who are considered rulers
over the Gentiles lord it over them, and their great
ones exercise authority over them. Yet it shall not
be so among you; but whoever desires to become
great among you shall be your servant. And whoever of you desires to be first shall be slave of all.
For even the Son of Man did not come to be
served, but to serve, and to give His life as ransom
for many" (Mark 10:42-45).*

The title of bishop is one of service, not of honor, and therefore a bishop should strive to serve others rather than lord it over them. Such is the precept of the Master.

HOMOTHUMADON—OF ONE ACCORD

An excellent example of the body of Christ working together as one unit with *agape* (love) and *koinonia* (con-cord) is expressed by a Greek word that appears eleven times in the New Testament. It is the word *homothu-madon*, which means "of one mind and purpose" or "of one accord". It is a word that describes the harmony and unanimity of the early church.

Following the Ascension of Jesus, we find the disci-ples gathered in prayer in the Upper Room "with one accord" (*homothumadon*). Following the Council of Jerusalem, St. Luke writes that the early Church was "of one accord" (*homothumadon*) in declaring the decision of the Council to Gentile believers in the Disaspora (Acts 15:25). When the church today works together as one body, one unit, clergy and laity in *syndiaconia* (synergy), it achieves *homothumadon*, the exemplary harmony and concord that existed in the early Church under the aegis of the Holy Spirit.

PART THREE

Syndiaconia: The Shared Role of the Hierarchy and Laity in the Church

Independence is not a Christian word; *interdependence* is.

Syndiaconia: serving together, working together, yoked together under the yoke of Christ as sanctified, consecrated, and chrismated members of His body, we labor to bring glory to God, the Father, the Son, and the Holy Spirit.

SYNDIACONIA: THE SHARED ROLE OF THE HIERARCHY AND LAITY IN THE CHURCH

In a Peanuts cartoon Lucy says to Linus, "Change the TV channel!" Linus says, "Why should I?" Lucy shows him her fist. "You see these five fingers. By themselves they are nothing, but together they form a formidable weapon." Linus says, "Which channel do you want?"

Linus then looks at his five fingers and says, "Why can't you get together and do something?"

As members of the same body of Christ, clergy and laity need to "get together and do something" for the Lord. There is wisdom and power in working together under the guidance of the Holy Spirit. The Great Commission— "Go, preach the Gospel to all the world"—entrusted by the Lord Jesus to the church is entrusted to the entire church, clergy and laity alike. "All of us are Christ's body and each one is a part of it" (1 Cor. 12:12-27). *Independence,* as has been stated, is not a Christian word; *interdependence* is! *Syndiaconia:* serving together, working together, yoked together under the same yoke of Christ, we are called upon to "get together and do something" for the Lord.

If, in the Church Militant, it is only the hierarchy and the clergy who fulfill the function of ministry, then it is like fighting a battle with only commissioned officers and generals. That is why we so desperately need *syndiaconia!*

St. Paul speaks of our pilgrimage on earth as running a race. What would happen in a marathon if only coaches ran the race while everyone else stayed home and watched it on television? Is not this much like the situation in the church today? For the most part the coaches run the race. Everyone else *attends*. We *attend* the liturgy. We *attend* classes. We *attend*, when we ought to be *participating*, *running* the race with the coaches. The coaches (the priests and bishops) can run alongside us, with us, encouraging us, advising us, but they cannot run for us. We are all running together. This is s*yndiaconia*!

Faith, like a child, matures best in a community of love. As members of Christ's Body, we are also members of each other. I am part of you, and you are part of me.

And I, as a priest, will grow in faith, or shrink in faith, in large measure as your love supports me, or as your love abandons me. St. Paul was right on target when he wrote that no Christian can say to any other Christian, "I have no need of you" (l Cor. 12:21). With any failure of love, I am diminished. In St. Paul's striking image of the body and its members, no member of the body can be insensitive to, or unaffected by, what happens to the rest of the body. We are incredibly one, all of us who feed upon the same Body and Blood of our Lord. *Syndiaconia*!

"When one member suffers, all the members suffer with him" (1 Cor. 12:26). This is said of the Church. If we do not feel as our own, the pain of another's suffering, then we are not within the Church. This brings us beyond *syndiaconia* to *synpascho*: I *feel*, I *experience* as my own, the pain, the sorrow, the heartache of my fellow member in the body of Christ—be he bishop, priest or lay person— and as I reach out to help, I do so in great humility and with the super-sensitive love of Christ so as not to diminish that person's dignity. "Now abide faith, hope and love, but the greatest of these is love."

Just as in the epiclesis prayer of the liturgy we call down the fire of the Holy Spirit to change the bread and the wine into the Body and Blood of Jesus, so at the same time and in the same prayer we call that same fire of the Holy Spirit upon ourselves, so that the same Holy Spirit who transforms the bread and the wine into the Body of Christ, may through the Eucharist transform us also into the Body of Christ, all of us, clergy and laity alike. "Christ is the head of the body (the Church)", writes St. Chrysostom, "but of what use is the head without hands, without feet, without eyes, without ears, without tongue?" "Everything is done by God, and yet nothing is done without us," someone said. We call it *Syndiaconia*.

Let us look now at some of the ways by which s*yndiaconia* has always been practiced in the Church.

THE PRESBYTER AND THE BISHOP

In *The Apostolic Constitutions* (II, 28), the presbyters are identified as "the bishop's counselors, the crown of the Church…the council and senate of the Church." In the *Antiquities of the Christian Church*, it is summed up this way: "Though the bishop was prince and head of the ecclesiastical senate, and nothing could regularly be done without him, yet neither did he ordinarily do any public act relating to government and discipline of the church, without their advice and assistance." Moreover, Canon 22, IVth Council of Carthage, forbade any bishop to ordain anyone without the advice of his clergy, so that through them and together with them (the presbyters), he might keep in touch accurately with the sense of the people in his parishes. This is s*yndiaconia*: bishops, presbyters and lay people working together in mutual love for the glory of God.

THE ORDINATION OF CLERGY: AXIOS!

As we know, while performed by a bishop, an ordination requires the consent of the whole people of God. Accordingly, at a certain point in the ordination service, the assembled congregation ratifies the ordination by proclaiming loudly AXIOS!, meaning WORTHY! In theory, if the lay people express their dissent, the ordination cannot take place.

Let me quote here from Bishop Kallistos Ware,

In the early church the bishop was elected by the people of the diocese, clergy and laity together. In Orthodoxy today it is usually the Governing Synod in each autocephalous Church which appoints bishops to vacant sees; but in some Churches— Antioch, for example, and Cyprus—a modified system of election still exists. The Moscow Council of 1917-18 laid down that henceforward bishops in the Russian Church should be elected by the clergy and laity.*

Fr. George Florovsky points out:

Moreover, a participation of the "people" in the

* *The Orthodox Church.* T. Ware. Penguin Books. London, England. 1963.,

ordination itself is required, and not only as reverent spectators who follow the prayers. The binding "Axios" is not merely an accompaniment, but also a witness, and an acceptance. The power to ordain is bestowed on bishops and on bishops alone. But it is given to them within the Church as to the pastors of a definite flock. And they can and should realize this power only in the sobornost of the Church and in agreement with the entire Body—namely, the priests and the people—and not in a "general" or "abstract" way. This means that the bishop should abide in the Church, and the Church in the bishop.**

Thus, the active participation of the lay people in the ordination of the clergy is part of the Sacred Tradition of the Orthodox Church which is so well characterized by the word *syndiaconia.*

THE ROLE OF THE LAITY IN SYNODS

The greatest treasure for the famous Russian religious thinker Alexis Khomiakov was his membership in the Church. Its ecclesiological problems, he believed, were not only a concern of the hierarchy but of every member, laity and clergy alike. He felt that infallibility, as conceived by the Western Church, was dividing the Kingdom of God on earth, the body of Christ, as had been the case for centuries. In 1848 the Eastern Patriarchs, as already

---

* *Creation and Redemption.* Nordland Press

noted, signed an Encyclical and sent it to Pope Pius IX. It stated that infallibility resides solely in the ecumenical fellowship of the Church, united together by mutual love, and that the guardianship of dogmas and of the purity of rites is entrusted, not to the hierarchy alone but to all members of the church, who constitute the body of Christ.

Metropolitan Emilianos of the Ecumenical Patriarchate supported Khomiakov when he wrote, "The laity also had a real place in the formulation and proclamation of the truth of salvation and the true faith in the synods of the Church. We were certainly not forgetting that at the Synod of the Apostles (Acts 15:22), the decisions were taken 'as it seemed good to the apostles, the presbyters and the whole church' and that the custom was long continued in the church of admitting a fair number of lay people to the synods to express their opinion. The Synods define doctrine in their own right "with the assistance of the Holy Spirit, *ipso et divino jure*"; the faithful people subsequently recognize these definitions as not exceeding their destination but as interpreting practically and formulating infallibly the truth.   Metropolitan Emilianos continues,

The synod is summoned to study the problems and the needs of the whole people. The laity should, therefore, know what is going on, and be well-informed…. The synod is not an assembly behind closed doors, secret and mysterious.

Orthodoxy has for this reason strongly reproached Western theology for having created a dichotomy

and separation between a "teaching" Church (clergy) and a "learning" Church (laity) ... between an "active" and a "passive" Church.

We must, however, distinguish very clearly between the function of bishops—"judges of the faith"—and that of the laity—"defenders of the faith". Among the bishops there is a certain charism to guarantee the faith in its authenticity, but the defense of the faith is the business of the whole community. The spirit of Truth dwells in the body of the baptized united by the bond of love.... At the heart of the mystery of this unanimity we find the fact that all the faithful together constitute an eucharistic community. They have the same root and the same center—Christ. The Eucharist establishes an authentic community among them, just as long ago the Sinai covenant created the people of Israel.

The eminent historian and theologian, Fr. Dimitrios Constantelos, states that *syndiaconia* existed between bishops and laity in the synods and councils of the early Church. He writes:

It was neither the apostles (the bishops) nor the presbyters (priests) by themselves, but the whole church that determined the council's actions and deliberations. It was nearly two centuries later, when, for several reasons, the Episcopal office emerged as the leading office, that bishops became

*either the only or the dominant participants in a
council. The earliest church councils, in which the
clergy and the laity both participated in imitation
of the apostolic church, were held during the second half of the second century in Asia Minor to
refute the misleading teachings of the Montanists.*

Thus, we see that in the early church—second century
A.D.—the bishops' teaching was not performed in isolation from the rest of the Church.

SYNDIACONIA IN THE LITURGY

Nowhere is *syndiaconia* more obvious than in the liturgy, as was stated previously. The very word liturgy—*leitourgia*—means a common, corporate action in which all
who are present are active participants. The prayers of the
liturgy are all in the plural "we". The priest calls upon the
people to pray, "Let *us* pray to the Lord", "Let *us* com-
mend ourselves to the Lord", etc. The prayer of consecration requires the *AMEN* of God's people. When the priest
blesses the congregation with "Peace be with you", the
congregation returns the blessing by saying, "And with
your spirit." Canon law requires that the priest not celebrate the liturgy alone but with the people and that the
priest with the people receive the Eucharist at every liturgy. Clergy and laity co-celebrate the Divine Liturgy in a
beautiful symphony of *syndiaconia*. The Orthodox liturgy
makes no sense for a spectator; it demands participation.
As the late Fr. Schmemann wrote:

*Not only the laity but the clergy as well have sim-
ply forgotten that in the Eucharist all are ordained
and all serve, each in his place, in the one liturgical action of the Church. Who is serving, in other
words, is not the clergy, and not even the clergy
with the laity, but the Church, which is constituted
and made manifest in all fullness by everyone
together.*

CLERICALISM

A word now about clericalism which obliterates the
concept of *syndiaconia* by associating the clergy with the
church and the laity with the world. The laity are often
called *kosmikoi* in Greek, i.e., "belonging to the world",
even though in baptism we are called to renounce the sin-
ful world. The Greek word *laikos*, layman, carries with it
connotations of passivity, of not belonging to the active,
clerical state of the church. As someone wrote, "For centuries theology was thought of as an exclusively clerical
task. But the time has come for a declericalization of theology, to return to the way it was in the early church. If
theology is, above all, the study of the saving truth, it is
needed by all members of the church, for it is their spiritual food." Let me state here that clericalism, which totally
contradicts Orthodox theology, did not exist in the early
church. It crept into the church in the fourth century.

In the world, the word "layman" means a second-class
citizen. For example, I am a "layman" in regard to law
because I have not passed the bar; thus, I am not allowed
to practice law. There is no place in the church for those

who cannot practice. I was pleased to see a sign once outside a church which read:

MINISTERS: all the members.
EQUIPPER: Rev. John Smith.

Fr. John Chrysavvgis is right when he says, "The lay
faithful are not passive members of the body of our
Lord—passengers being blindly led by the driver—clergy,
or at most, some kind of back-seat drivers." We need to
realize that the monk who keeps vigil in Church praying in
a night service is not superior in holiness to the mother
who is kept awake all night by her crying baby who might
yet one day become a St. Basil, as Professor Tsirintanes,
former Professor of Law at the University of Athens,
maintained.

The mother who cares for her sick baby all night is
just as "priestly" and "holy" as the monk who prays all
night.

The distinction between lay people (*kosmikoi*) or
worldly ones, and the *klirikoi,* the clergy, is further obliter-
ated when we remember that the monks themselves are a
lay movement. Monks are not ordained clergy. Bishop
Ware explains that "in the Orthodox Church it is not
entirely unknown for a layman to act as a spiritual father;
but in that case, while he hears the confession, gives
advice, and assures the penitent of God's forgiveness, he
does not pronounce the prayer of sacramental absolution
but sends the penitent to the priest." It is a beautiful
expression of *syndiaconia.*

Another strong refutation of clericalism in the Orthodox Church consists in the fact that according to Orthodox tradition the whole people of God share in the prophetic—or teaching—role of Christ as well. The great tradition of monastic teaching is a case in point. The widespread practice of lay theology professors in Orthodox schools of theology is an outgrowth of this ecclesiological truth. More specifically, the laity, always under the guidance of the clergy and especially the bishop, teach others and themselves. Parents who teach their children the catechism as well as Sunday school teachers, lay writers of religious books, all share in Christ's teaching ministry as members of the spiritual priesthood of the Church. And each believer, as he or she expends effort to learn the faith, attends classes, counsels and advises neighbors, relatives and friends, is a participant in the prophetic-teaching role of the Church.

This is the deep meaning of *syndiaconia*. In the words of Fr. Afanasieff, "The differentiation in the Body of Christ is not ontological but functional. Ontologically, all members of the Church are 'laymen', belonging to the Holy People of God. Therefore, any form of clericalism (the idea that only the clergy or even one bishop can represent the church) changes the very nature of the church."

A parishioner said to a priest one day, "Did you visit so-and-so in the hospital?"

The priest replied, "Yes. Did you?"

The purpose of the ordained priesthood is to prepare more spiritual fathers and mothers in the church who will reach out with the priest to do the work of ministry.

Christ does not want the members of His body to be a

community of robots. He called us to be "salt", "light" and "yeast", called to transform the world.

THE BISHOP AND HIS PEOPLE

It is proper for the bishop to consult with the elders of his people before making important decisions. This is not democracy, but something that belongs to the essence of the church. The church is not the clergy, but the bishop with his people. Even Cyprian who said "that the bishop is in the church and the church in the bishop" also said: "They are the church who are a people united to the priest, and the flock which adheres to its shepherd." The royal priesthood includes clergy and laity—together they comprise the Body of Christ; together they realize the mystery of Christ; together they live out the life of Christ.

It is crucial to preserve a balance between the royal priesthood of the laity to which all baptized are ordained and the ministry of the ordained clergy. This is the delicate and beautiful balance of *syndiaconia*.

Fr. George Florovsky addressed this point:

Again, the power of the hierarchy does not assume that truth, as it were, is revealed automatically to the bishop, by force of his ordination and dignity, or that he can discover it without consultation and communion with that Church outside of which he loses all "power", generally speaking. However, only to him, and to him alone, is given the right to speak in a Catholic way. It is not only a canonical privilege or right. It is bound up with the fact that

the bishop as such is a mystical center of his flock,
which unites in him in the oneness of sacramental
fellowship...even laymen can and must study, dis-
cuss, preach, write, and argue; they can similarly
disagree with bishops. But to witness on behalf of
the Church is given only to the bishop. One can
also put it thus: the right of an opinion and of
advice is given to all, but the "power to teach" is
bestowed on the hierarchy alone—of course, in the
unbreakableness of soborny fellowship.... For the
voice of laymen must be heard in the Orthodox
choir. The leader of the choir, however, can only
be a bishop. There are various gifts, and all gifts
are necessary. Only one, however, is appointed
shepherd and the staff is entrusted to him. "And
the sheep follow him: for they know His voice"
(John 10:4).

Bishops have an essential role in the constitution of the
church as Father John Behr wrote,

Yet their essential role should not be overstated, it
is not by virtue of being gathered around the bish-
op that a community is the church, but by virtue of
Christ himself; as Ignatius puts it, in words which
are often misquoted: "Whenever the bishop
appears, let the congregation be present, just as
wherever Christ is, there is the catholic Church"
(Letter to the Smrynaeans 8). It is Christ who
makes the congregation to be his body, the Church,
and so when Ignatius writes his letters, he does so

to the whole community, not to the bishop, warning them to "be deaf when anyone speaks to you apart from Jesus Christ" (Letter to the Trallians 9).*

THE LAYPERSON IN ORTHODOX THEOLOGY

There is not just one priesthood. There is the "royal priesthood" of all the baptized and the special priesthood of the ordained clergy. It is unfortunate that a lay person has come to mean a nonprofessional in whatever field. It is assumed that the important work in any field is done not by the layman but by the professional.

This is a far cry from the meaning of the word layman in the early Church. Coming from the word *laos* which means *people*, it refers to the people of God, the Israelites, chosen and sanctified by God Himself as *His* people to serve Him in a special way. In Christ, the church, i.e., those who believe in Him and are baptized, become the new Israel, the new people of God—again, called and consecrated by God to serve Him in a special way.

One cannot read the Old Testament without realizing God's effort to shape a distinctive people among the nations that is so dedicated to serving God as to become "a light to the Gentiles". The twelve apostles chosen by Jesus represented the twelve tribes of Israel, the People of God. The word *laos* from which the word laity is derived, is applied to the People of God, to Israel, and now to the new Israel, the Church. Thus, the word layman (from *laos*, the People of God) is an exalted title expressing our

* *The Trinitarian Being of the Church.* Fr. John Behr. St. Vladimir's Theological Quarterly. Vol . 48. 2004.

choseness by God and our common vocation to declare the marvelous deeds of Him Who redeemed us.

In the practice of the Orthodox Church each Christian is ordained into the *laos,* the laity, the People of God, through Baptism and Chrismation. Whereas Baptism restores in us the image of God, obscured by sin, Chrismation, our personal Pentecost, gives us the power of the Holy Spirit to be Christians, responsible participants in the life and work of the church.

Thus, the word lay or *laikos* is given a highly positive meaning. Moses said to the people of the covenant: "You are a holy people to the Lord your God. The Lord your God has chosen you to be a people of his own possession, out of all the people that are on the face of the earth." St. Paul calls all baptized Christians, "fellow citizens with the saints and members of the household of God" (Eph. 2:1). Addressing himself to the early Christians, St. Peter said, "But you are a chosen race, a royal priesthood, a holy nation, God's own people, that you may declare the wonderful deeds of him who called you out of darkness into his marvelous light. Once you were no people; once you had not received mercy, but now you have received mercy" (1 Peter 2:9-10). Clergy need to keep reminding lay people of their high calling. If they are members of St. Nicholas Church or St. George Church, St. Peter says, they are "members of a chosen race, a royal priesthood, a holy nation, God's own people." This is the layman's identity; this is who he is. Having defined identity, St. Peter proceeds to give the layman his/her job description: "to declare the wonderful deeds of him who called you out of the darkness into his marvelous light".

THE PRIESTHOOD OF THE LAITY

We read in the Homilies of St. Macarius these words addressed to lay people:

Do you not realize or understand your own nobility? Each of those who have been anointed with the heavenly chrism becomes a Christ by grace, so that all are kings and prophets of the heavenly mysteries.

Elsewhere he writes,

Recognize your nobility, your royalty...your priesthood. You are prophets of the heavenly mysteries...sons and lords and gods.

Alcuin wrote,

In Old Testament times only kings and priests received a mystical anointing. But after our Lord, the true king and eternal priest, had been anointed by God, the heavenly Father, with this mystical unction, it was no longer only kings and priests but the whole church that was consecrated with the anointing of Chrism, because every person in the church is a member of the eternal King and Priest. Because we are a royal and priestly nation, we are anointed after the washing of baptism, that we may be bearers of the name of Christ.

Metropolitan Emilianos adds, "At no point of dogma are the Fathers more completely unanimous than on the priesthood of the laity."

The ascetics themselves recognized that holiness is inherent in the laity. In *The Sayings of the Desert Fathers* we find the following story about St. Antony, the greatest of solitaries: "It was revealed to Abba Antony in the desert: In the city there is someone who is your equal, a doctor by profession. Whatever he has to spare he gives to those in need, and all day long he sings the Thrice-Holy Hymn with the angels." Antony was directed by God to visit a layman, a physician, who was equal to him in sanctity!

PAUL EVDOKIMOV ON THE ROYAL PRIEST-HOOD OF THE BAPTIZED

Paul Evdokimov has this to say about the royal priesthood of the believers:

> *The anointing (1 John 2:20), formerly reserved for kings, priests, and prophets, is extended in the Church to all believers. It is no longer the ethnic element (Israel) or the spatial (the temple of Jerusalem) that constitutes the body (John 4:21-24); it is Christ who unites in Himself all those baptized "into the people of God", where everyone is a layperson, belonging to "the priestly people".... It is not a question of "priest" in the sense of "a presbyter" and of his sacramental power (the bishop). A priest of the royal priesthood(every*

believer) is one who participates in the Priesthood of Christ, not through his sacred functions but by virtue of his sanctified being. It is in view of this ontological sacerdotal dignity that each baptized person is sealed with the gifts, "anointed by the Spirit" in his very being. Attention must be drawn to the priestly being of every believer. This means that the believer offers the totality of his life and being as a sacrifice, that he makes of his life a liturgy. *

THE TWOFOLD WORK OF MINISTRY

The work of ministry is twofold: to gather together the people of God for worship, instruction and empowering, and then to scatter them into the world as servants of Christ. We not only go to Church, we are the Church wherever we go. The true liturgy begins when we leave Church to celebrate "the liturgy after the liturgy". The task of the ordained clergy is to so train the people of God that they may enter the world to show forth the love of God and the justice of God. The particular priesthood of the ordained clergy exists in order to train and develop the universal priesthood of the people of God.

THE CHURCH IS NOT "THEY" BUT "WE"

We have often heard the Church referred to as "*they*". "They" should do this "They" should do that. "They"

* *Sacrament of Love.* Paul Evdokimov. SVS Press. Scarsdale, N.Y. 1985

should be more interested in young people. "They" should be more active in helping persons in need. Granted, "they" is a very convenient way of getting oneself off the hook, but it also lays bare a serious sickness in the church. Many lay people do not feel that they are part of the church. The church is always someone else: the archbishop, the bishop, the priest, or the parish council. What could be more deadly to any group than to have its adherents feel that they are not involved, not part of the group, not a member of the body?

PROFESSIONAL SPECTATORS

A reporter asked Bud Wilkinson, former football coach at the University of Oklahoma and former director of the President's Physical Fitness Program, "What would you say is the contribution of modern football to physical fitness?"

Wilkinson flashed, "Absolutely nothing!"

"Would you care to elaborate?" asked the nonplussed reporter.

"Certainly," replied Wilkinson. "I define football as twenty-two men on the field desperately needing rest and forty thousand people in the stands desperately needing exercise!"

How applicable to the average church is this appraisal of modern football. The overwhelming majority of people in the church are nonparticipating spectators at ease in God's Zion. We have developed a spectator Christianity. Professional spectators, by the way, almost always turn into critics. The football fan becomes the Monday morning quarterback. If it is true that the most effective way of learning is by doing, then the spectators who are doing nothing are learning nothing. This is why we need to re-capture and implement the concept of *syndiaconia* which is so much a part of our Orthodox tradition.

I conclude with these words from St. Paul. In his Letter to the Colossians, St. Paul calls on us to be what we are: the people of God: the royal priesthood of believers, working together in *syndiaconia*, clergy and laity alike:

> *You are the people of God; He loved you and chose you for His own. Therefore you must put on compassion, kindness, humility, gentleness, and patience. Be helpful to one another, and forgive one another, whenever any of you has a complaint against someone else. You must forgive each other in the same way that the Lord has forgiven you. And to all these add love, which binds all things together in perfect unity. The peace that Christ gives is to be the judge in your hearts; for to this peace God has called you together in one body. And be thankful. Christ's message, in all its richness, must live in your hearts" (Col. 3:12-16).*

> *Now to him who by the power at work within us is able to accomplish abundantly far more than all we can ask or imagine, to him be glory in the church and in Christ Jesus to all generations, forever and ever. Amen. (Eph. 3:20-21)*